Beadwoven Glamour

CRYSTAL-EMBELLISHED JEWELRY

Kalmbach
Media

Dedication

I dedicate this book to my irreplaceable father, Aurel Klein, who left me on March 22, 2018, after fighting a long and painful illness. Thank you for being a part of my life. I will always carry you in my heart and miss you.

To my wonderful daughter, Shani Lam, who changed my life forever and makes me a better person every day. To my husband, Avi Lam, who believes in me and encourages me to share my passion for beading with lots of love. Thank you both for believing in me and for your endless support throughout the process.

Kalmbach Books
A division of Kalmbach Media
21027 Crossroads Circle
Waukesha, Wisconsin 53186
www.JewelryAndBeadingStore.com

Published in 2019
23 22 21 20 19   1 2 3 4 5

Manufactured in China

ISBN: 978-1-62700-565-4
EISBN: 978-1-62700-566-1

Editor: Erica Barse
Book Design: Lisa Schroeder
Technical Editors: Jane Danley Cruz, Julia Gerlach
Photographer: William Zuback
Copy Editor: Dianne Wheeler

Library of Congress Control Number: 2018944522

Contents

Introduction

I invite you to join my unique and private world of beads. Almost ten years have passed since I began to look back and understand how all the small events, just like the variety of beads, made the story of my life. Bead after bead and event following event, the designs I have created reflect who I am and tell the story of my life. Over the last ten years, I found myself pulled deeper and deeper into the world of beads, creating lovely designs with colorful and magical baubles. Through these designs, I learn who I am and the way I am defined.

I believe there is a reason for everything, and if you don't succeed today, you must try again and again. In life, we collect events and experiences the same way we collect the variety of beads with which we create a better and more beautiful world. Our newly created world gives us motivation to keep on going.

The world of beads is my way to create something from nothing. The satisfaction from creating for me is firstly from my personal joy. Secondly, I love the many compliments my students receive when they create a necklace, bracelet, or pendant with my guidance.

The magic world of beads still burns in me and through this book, I hope to pass it on to you. In happy moments as in sad ones, in moments full of excitement and joy, beading has proved to have healing qualities. Beading offers therapy and personal growth, not in the medical sense, but through doing: physical therapy, as it were. Beading pulls us inside and allows us to depart, even for a short time, from our everyday routine.

Beading gives the soul a blessed rest and a chance to relax. There are some people who will climb mountains. When they reach the peak, they feel full of adrenaline and accomplishment. For me, every piece I make is a peak filled with pride, joy, and the desire to create more.

I want to share the peaks with you, learning together what more can be done to discover the next beauty. I believe that the secret of success is the will—and where there is a will, there is a pathway. If you have the desire and the will, you can do it!

Detailed instructions will enable you as a beader to challenge yourself and fulfill your dream to design jewelry that goes beyond fashion and trends.

Together, we will go on a journey. I will show you how to create a variety of beaded jewelry pieces using basic techniques with a nice twist. These designs will complement you and allow you to showcase your personal touch—all with tiny magical and sparkling beads.

Believe in me and believe in yourself. So, let's start!

— Isabella

Basics

MATERIALS

There are just a handful of materials you will need to complete the beautiful projects in this book: Beads of many shapes and sizes, beading needles, and beading thread. I prefer Swarovski beads and components, Miyuki glass seed beads, and Czech pressed glass beads. However, you can substitute your favorite beads where desired.

CRYSTALS

Swarovski offers the highest standard available on the market. The high-quality precision cutting and the clear through-hole achieve high brilliance and clarity. Rounded hole edges reduce the wear on thread and increase the durability of designs. As a unique feature, they possess a polished hole that creates even more brilliance and color intensity. A wide range of colors and effects opens up endless possibilities for different combinations and designs. Here's a brief introduction to the crystals you'll use in this book.

Bicones
Swarovski Article 5328

Bicones

Bicone crystals are my favorite crystal beads. I use 3mm and 4mm Swarovski bicone crystals in a variety of colors, coatings, and effects to create my favorite pieces.

Briolettes

These brilliant, fully-cut Swarovski **briolette** crystals exude timeless elegance. I combine 13mm and 15mm pendants in many of my designs. I love the shiny movement they add to any jewelry design. Using them is particularly easy because of the "crystal clear hole" with rounded edges.

Briolettes
Swarovski Article 6012

Chaton
Swarovski Article 1088

Fancy oval stone
Swarovski Article 4127

Chatons, fancy oval stones, and rivolis

Due to their round fronts (with a flat surface) and pointed backs, **chatons** are easy to use in your jewelry designs. A **fancy oval stone** can be added to beadwork in the same way; it transforms each design into something unforgettable (I love the 22x30mm size). A **rivoli** is a round stone that comes to a point on both sides. Their unique facets and one-sided foiling refract light in a dazzling display. All of these crystal stones add instant flash to any project.

Navettes, rose montées, and set-in stones

These are highly effective combinations of metal and integrated Swarovski crystals. **Navettes** are wonderful for making jewelry designs with a bit of an edge. A **rose montée** is a sew-on rhinestone with a metal channel attached to the back. This channel is in the shape of a criss cross. **Set-in stones**, with straight channels, can be sewn through as well.

Rivolis
Swarovski Article 1122

Navettes
Swarovski Article 13304

Rose montées
Swarovski Article 53103

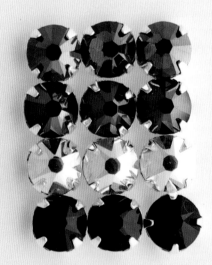

Set-in stones
Swarovski Article 17704

GLASS BEADS

Seed beads

"Seed bead" is a generic term for any small bead. There are various types, such as **round** and **3.4mm drop** (found in this book), as well as cylinder (Delica), hexagon, bugle, triangle, and more. I like to use Miyuki glass seed beads from Japan, which are considered a "world standard" for their high quality, brilliance, and uniform shape. Seed beads are used in many ways to create beaded jewelry. You will find them in all of my projects.

Shaped beads

I love Czech pressed glass beads, which are formed by pressing a heated glass rod into a mold. These beads come in many versatile shapes, sizes, styles, and colors.

Some beads have only one hole, such as **drop beads** (either top-drilled or with a vertical hole), **dagger beads** (large and small), **Tulip petals**, and **O-Beads**. You can also find shiny glass **pearls** and **fire-polished beads** in various shapes and finishes, as well as larger shapes, such as pressed glass **leaf beads**.

Round seed beads
8º, 11º, and 15º

Drops
3.4mm

Dagger beads
3x10mm and 5x16mm

Drop beads, top-drilled
5x7mm and 6x9mm

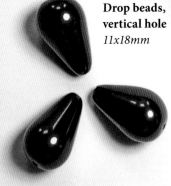

Drop beads, vertical hole
11x18mm

Glass pearls
3mm, 4mm, 6mm, 8mm

Tulip petals
6x8mm

O-Beads
1x4mm

Fire-polished beads, round
4mm

Pressed glass leaf beads, side hole
13x18mm

Multi-hole beads

SuperDuo beads, **MiniDuo beads**, **Rulla beads**, **Silky beads**, and **Vexolo beads** all have two holes. **GemDuo beads** have a back and a front, so pay attention while picking them up in your design! Paisley-shaped **ZoliDuo beads** are available in two versions: left and right.

Crescent-like **Arcos par Puca beads** have three holes, and the interesting, V-shaped **AVA beads** have a hole in the tip and in each side. With so many unique beads to choose from, your design possibilities are nearly endless!

SuperDuo beads
2x5mm

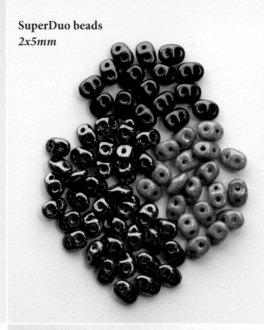

MiniDuo beads
2x4mm

Rulla beads
3x5mm

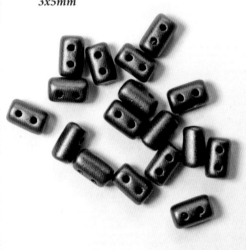

Silky beads
6mm

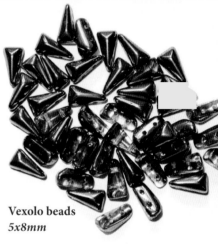

Vexolo beads
5x8mm

Arcos par Puca beads
5x10mm

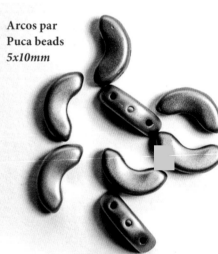

GemDuo beads
5x8mm

ZoliDuo beads, left and right version
5x8mm

AVA beads
4x10mm

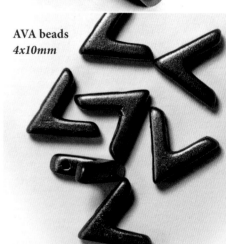

BASIC TOOLKIT For every project in this book, you will need a few supplies.

Scissors
A good pair of sharp scissors will cut the threads closer to the stitched design's end point easily.

Thread
Make sure the thread is strong. I recommend Fireline beading thread or a similar 0.15mm/6-lb. test thread, such as Dandyline. You are making beautiful jewelry; it needs to last!

Tape measure
Use this to measure your wrist, neck, or beadwork.

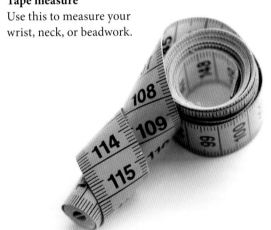

Thread burner
Also called a "thread zapper," this tool melts the end of a thread next to a knot

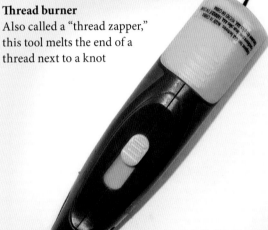

Needles
I use size 12 beading needles when working with very small beads/seed beads—especially when making multiple passes through beads.

Beading mat
Use a beading mat to keep beads from rolling all over the table.

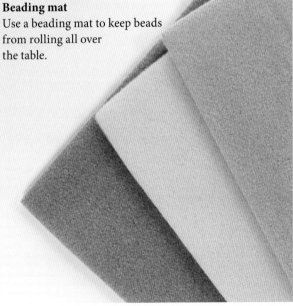

TECHNIQUES

Starting Your Work

Start with a comfortable thread length. I recommend about 1½ yd. (about 1.4m) for starting. String a stopper bead, leaving about a 4-in. (10cm) tail. Sew through the stopper bead twice to anchor the bead. (A stopper bead is an 11º round seed bead in a different color from those you are working with. You will remove this bead at the end of your work or earlier if mentioned otherwise).

DON'T FORGET!
Never use the same thread you used in your beading project to attach the clasp. Use a new thread. This will allow you to replace the clasp in case it gets broken. You can also extend your beadwork to fit better without needing to re-work parts of it.

Adding thread
Usually I tie a half-hitch knot with the new thread into the work a few beads before the end of the thread. The knot should be between two beads. Continue through the beads in the same path that the old thread is exiting. Only then will you finish the old thread.

Finishing thread
Never cut the thread near the knot point. The knot point is a weak point and can come undone. After attaching the new thread between two beads with a double half-hitch knot, I recommend taking the short tail left and passing it back through the beads (at least 2 in./5cm) before cutting.

Finishing your beadwork
Finish all threads before adding the clasp. Try to leave the beads you will attach the clasp to free from threads as much as possible.

Stitching Techniques

Surgeon's knot

1 Cross one end of the thread over and under the other twice. Pull both ends to tighten the first half of the knot.

2 Cross the first end of the thread over and under the other end. Pull both ends to tighten the knot.

Half-hitch knot
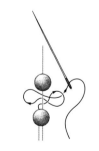

Pass the needle under the thread bridge between two beads, and pull gently until a loop forms. Cross back over the thread between the beads, sew through the loop, and pull gently to draw the knot into the beadwork.

Ladder stitch

1 Pick up two beads, and sew through them both again, positioning the beads side by side so that their holes are parallel (a–b).

2 Add subsequent beads by picking up one bead, sewing through the previous bead, then sewing through the new bead (b–c). Continue for the desired length.

Peyote stitch, flat even-count

1 Pick up an even number of beads, leaving the desired length of tail (**a–b**). These beads will shift to form the first two rows as the third row is added.

2 To begin row 3, pick up a bead, skip the last bead added in the previous step, and sew back through the next bead, working toward the tail (**b–c**). For each stitch, pick up a bead, skip a bead in the previous row, and sew through the next bead until you reach the first bead picked up in step 1 (**c–d**). The beads added in this row are higher than the previous rows and are referred to as "up-beads."

3 For each stitch in subsequent rows, pick up a bead, and sew through the next up-bead in the previous row (**d–e**). To count peyote stitch rows, count the total number of beads along both straight edges.

Herringbone stitch

Flat strip

1 Work the first row in ladder stitch (see "Ladder stitch") to the desired length using an even number of beads, and exit the top of the last bead added.

2 Pick up two beads, and sew down through the next bead in the previous row (**a–b**) and up through the following bead in the previous row. Repeat (**b–c**) across the first row.

3 To turn to start the next row, sew back through the last bead of the pair just added (**a–b**).

4 To work the next row, pick up two beads, sew down through the next bead in the previous row and up through the following bead (**b–c**). Continue adding pairs of beads across the row.

To turn without having thread show on the edge, pick up an accent or smaller bead before you sew back through the last bead of the pair you just added.

Right-angle weave

Flat strip

1 To start the first row of right-angle weave, pick up four beads, and tie them into a ring.
Sew through the first three beads again.

2 Pick up three beads. Sew through the last bead in the previous stitch (**a–b**), and continue through the first two beads picked up in this stitch (**b–c**).

3 Continue adding three beads per stitch until the first row is the desired length. You are stitching in a figure-8 pattern, alternating the direction of the thread path for each stitch.

Forming a strip into a ring

Exit the end bead of the last stitch, pick up a bead, and sew through the end bead of the first stitch. Pick up a bead, and sew through the end bead of the last stitch. Retrace the thread path to reinforce the join.

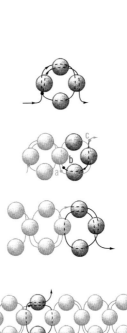

Projects

Rascal Bracelet

SUPPLIES

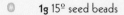

- **1g** 15º seed beads
- **2g** 11º seed beads
- **4g** 8º seed beads
- **14** Rulla beads
- **24** 3mm bicone crystals
- **12** 5mm bicone crystals
- **28** ZoliDuo beads, right version
- **28** ZoliDuo beads, left version
- **14** GemDuo beads
- **7** 7x15mm navettes
- **6** 8mm (SS29) set-in stones, Swarovski 17704
- 3-loop or box clasp
- Beading needle and thread

"Give a girl the right jewelry and she can conquer the world."

— Marilyn Monroe

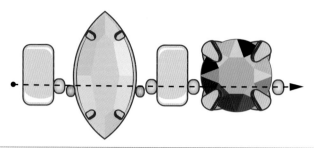

1 Thread a needle on a comfortable length of thread, and pick up a Rulla, 8º seed bead, 11º seed bead, navette, 11º, 8º, Rulla, 8º, 8mm set-in stone, and 8º. Repeat this stitch until you reach your desired length. Finish with a Rulla, 8º, 11º, navette, 11º, 8º, and Rulla.

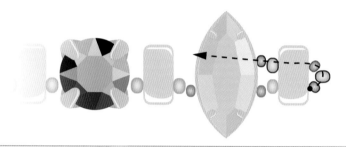

2 Pick up an 11º, 8º, and 11º. Sew through the free hole of the end Rulla. Pick up an 8º and an 11º. Sew through the free hole of the adjacent navette.

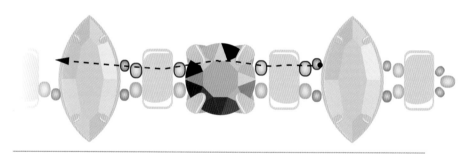

3 A. Pick up an 11º and 8º. Sew through the free hole of the next Rulla.
B. Pick up an 8º. Sew through the free hole of the next 8mm set-in stone.
C. Pick up an 8º. Sew through the free hole of the next Rulla.
D. Pick up an 8º and an 11º. Sew through the free hole of the next navette, as shown.
E. Repeat A–D to the end of the bracelet, ending and adding thread as needed. Finish by exiting the last Rulla.

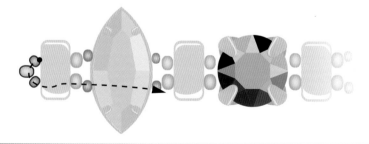

4 At the end, pick up an 11º, 8º, and 11º. Sew through the other hole of the end Rulla. Continue through the next 8º, 11º, navette, and 11º, as shown.

14

5 A. Pick up an 8º, ZoliDuo (left, concave side), GemDuo, Zoli-Duo (right, convex side), and 8º. (Make sure the two-hole beads are facing up!) Sew through the adjacent 11º, navette, 11º, 8º, Rulla, and 8º.
B. Pick up four 11ºs, and sew through the following 8º, Rulla, 8º, 11º, navette, and 11º, as shown.
C. Repeat 5A and B for the length of the bracelet, exiting the last Rulla.

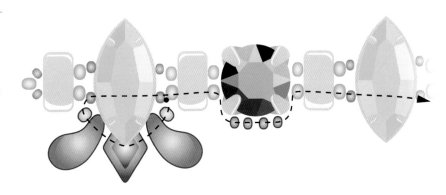

6 Sew through the end 11º, 8º, 11º, Rulla, 8º, 11º, navette, and 11º.
A. Pick up an 8º, ZoliDuo (left), GemDuo, ZoliDuo (right), and 8º. Sew through the adjacent 11º, navette, and 11º again. Continue through the next 8º, Rulla, and 8º.
B. Pick up four 11ºs. Skip the next 8mm set-in stone, and sew through the following 8º, Rulla, 8º, 11º, navette, and 11º, as shown.

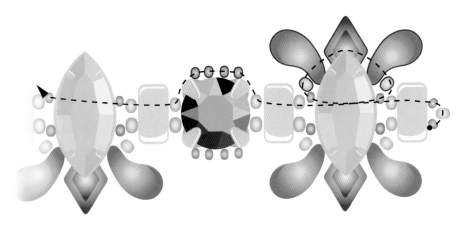

7 Repeat 6A and B for the length of the bracelet. Finish by exiting the last Rulla.

8 A. Sew through the end 11º, 8º, 11º, Rulla, and 8º.
B. Pick up a 15º seed bead. Sew through the next 8º.
C. Pick up four 15ºs, and sew through the free hole of the next ZoliDuo.
D. Pick up a ZoliDuo (right) and an 8º. Sew through the free hole of the adjacent GemDuo.
E. Pick up an 8º and a ZoliDuo (left). Sew through the free hole of the next ZoliDuo.
F. Pick up an 11º and a 3mm bicone crystal. Sew through the second and third 11ºs in the next set of four 11ºs added in the previous step.
G. Pick up a 3mm bicone crystal and an 11º. Sew through the free hole of the next ZoliDuo.
H. Repeat 8D–G to the end of the bracelet. Finish at step 8E.

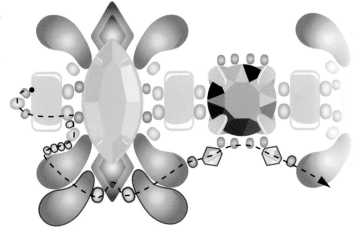

9 A. Pick up four 15ºs. Sew through the next 8º, as shown.
B. Pick up a 15º. Sew through the next 8º, Rulla, 11º, 8º, and 11º. Continue through the other hole of the Rulla and the following 8º.
C. Pick up a 15º. Sew through the next 8º.
D. Pick up four 15ºs. Sew through the free hole of the adjacent ZoliDuo.

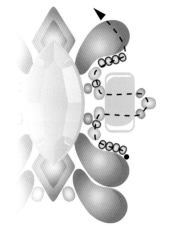

10 Repeat steps 8D–G for the remainder of the bracelet. Finish at step 8E.

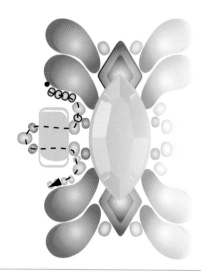

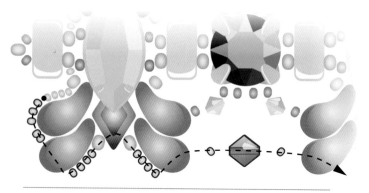

11 A. At the end, pick up four 15ºs. Sew through the next 8º.
B. Pick up a 15º. Sew through the marked beads. Finish by exiting four 15ºs.

12 A. Pick up five 15ºs. Sew through the free hole of the next outer ZoliDuo.
B. Pick up four 15ºs. Sew through the next 8º, GemDuo, and 8º.
C. Pick up four 15ºs. Sew through the free hole of the next outer ZoliDuo.
D. Pick up a 15º, 5mm bicone crystal, and 15º. Sew through the free hole of the next outer ZoliDuo.
E. Repeat steps 12B–D to the end of the bracelet.

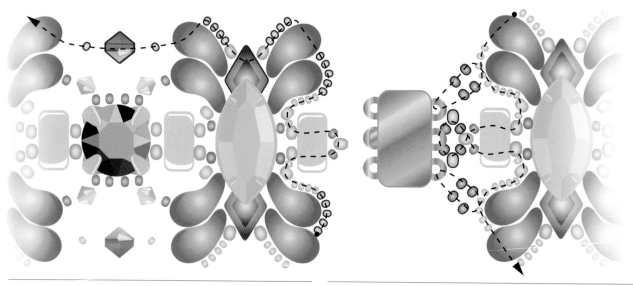

13 A. At the end: Pick up five 15ºs. Sew through the marked beads. Finish by exiting the four 15ºs on the other side of the bracelet.
B. Pick up five 15ºs. Sew through the free hole of the next outer ZoliDuo.
C. Pick up four 15ºs. Sew through the next 8º, GemDuo, and 8º.
D. Pick up four 15ºs. Sew through the free hole of the next outer ZoliDuo.
E. Pick up a 15º, 5mm bicone crystal, and 15º. Sew through the free hole of the next outer ZoliDuo. Repeat steps 13C–E for the remainder of the bracelet. Finish the thread.

14 Attach a new thread about 10 in. (25cm) long, and exit the fourth 15º at one end as shown.
A. Pick up two 11ºs, the first loop of the clasp, and two 11ºs. Sew through the previous two 15ºs. Sew through all the beads again to reinforce the thread. Continue through the beads to exit the 11º and 8º next to the Rulla.
B. Pick up an 11º, 8º, and 11º. Sew through the second loop of the clasp. Pick up an 11º, 8º, and 11º. Sew back through the 8º you first exited. Sew through all the beads again to reinforce the clasp connection. Continue through the marked beads, exiting seven 15ºs.
C. Pick up two 11ºs, the third loop of the clasp, and two 11ºs. Sew through the previous two 15ºs. Sew through all the beads again to reinforce the thread. Then sew through the sixth and the seventh 15ºs you just exited. Continue through the beads, and finish the thread.
D. Repeat A–C on the other end of the bracelet.

Bunnie
Necklace

SUPPLIES

- **4g** 15º seed beads
- **15g** 11º seed beads
- **17g** 8º seed beads
- **84** 3mm pearls
- **140** 3mm bicone crystals

- **11** 8mm (SS39) chatons
- **12** 14mm crystal rivolis
- **1** hook-and-eye clasp

Beading needle and thread

"No one understands and appreciates the hard work of beautiful design better than the designer."

—Isabella

1 Thread a needle on a comfortable length of thread, and pick up a 3mm pearl and an 11º seed bead seven times. Close the beads to a circle. Tie a surgeon's knot. Sew through the nearest 11º.

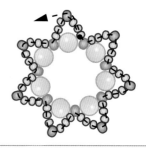

2 Pick up three 15º seed beads, an 11º, and three 15ºs. Sew through the next 11º. Repeat around the ring. Finish by stepping up through three 15ºs and an 11º.

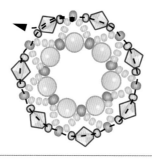

3 Pick up a 15º, 3mm bicone crystal, and 15º. Sew through the next 11º. Repeat around the ring. Finish by exiting a 3mm bicone crystal.

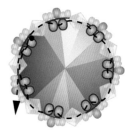

4 Insert a 14mm rivoli into the beadwork, face up. Pick up two 11ºs. Sew through the next 3mm bicone. Repeat around the ring. Sew through all the beads once more to reinforce. Finish by exiting an outer 11º.

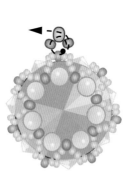

5 Pick up an 11º, 8º seed bead, and 11º. Sew through the 11º you first exited. Continue through the first 11º and 8º just added.

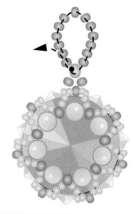

6 Pick up 13 11ºs. Sew through the 8º you first exited. Sew through all the beads again to reinforce the loop. Continue through the next two 11ºs.

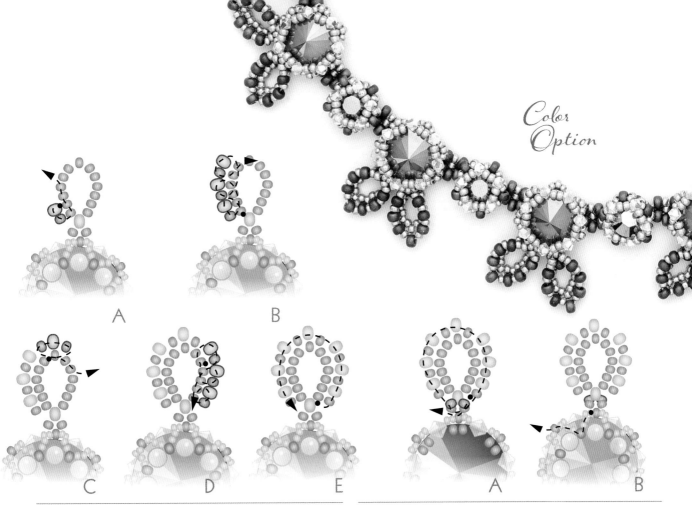

A   B

C   D   E   A   B

7 **A.** Pick up an 8º and an 11º. Sew through the same two 11ºs. Continue through the next two 11ºs as shown.
B. Repeat 7A twice.
C. Exit the seventh 11º in the loop. Pick up an 11º, 8º, and 11º. Sew through the seventh 11º again, and continue through the next two 11ºs.
D. Pick up an 11º and an 8º. Sew through the same two 11ºs. Continue through the next two 11ºs. Repeat this step twice.
E. Sew through all the beads you added in steps 7A–D.

8 **A.** Pick up an 11º. Sew through the 11º your thread exited at the start of step 5. Pick up another 11º. Sew through all the beads added in steps 7A–D. Pull the thread to curve the loop.
B. Continue through the marked beads (back view). Finish by exiting the marked 11º.

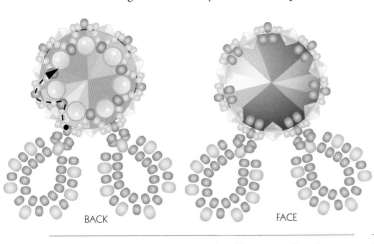

BACK   FACE

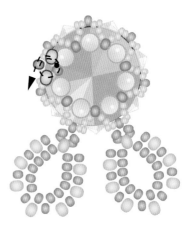

9 Repeat steps 5–8 to create another "bunny ear," ending and adding thread as needed. Finish by exiting the marked 11º, located between two pearls on the back.

10 Pick up an 8º, 11º, and 8º. Sew through the 11º you first exited. Continue through the first 8º and 11º just added.

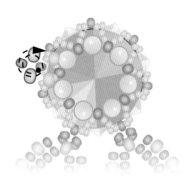

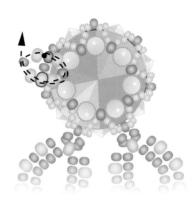

11 Pick up an 8º, 11º, and 8º. Sew through the 11º you first exited. Continue through all the beads added in this step.

12 Pick up an 11º, sew through the next 8º. Continue through the adjacent 11º and the next 8º on the other side. Pick up an 8º. Sew through the marked beads. Finish by exiting the marked 11º.

13 Pick up a repeating pattern of an 8º and two 11ºs four times, and then pick up another 8º and an 11º. Sew through the 11º you first exited and the following six beads to exit a pair of 11ºs.

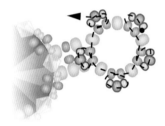

14 Pick up a 15º, 11º, and 15º. Sew through the same two 11ºs. Continue through the next 8º and following two 11ºs. Repeat this step around the ring. Step up through a 15º and an 11º.

15 Place an 8mm chaton in the newly-created ring, face up. Pick up a 15º, 3mm bicone crystal, and 15º. Sew through the next 11º. Repeat around. Finish by exiting a 3mm bicone crystal.

16 Pick up two 11ºs. Sew through the next 3mm bicone crystal. Repeat around the ring. Finish by exiting two 11ºs, and sew to the back side. Set this motif aside.

17 A. Position the new motif next to the previous one, making sure the bunny ears on both are pointing down and the back surfaces are facing up. You will attach the motifs so that there are two 8ºs above the connection points on the 8mm chaton and three pearls above the connection points on the 12mm rivoli. On the new motif, sew through the beadwork to exit the fourth 11º from the previous connection.
B. Pick up an 8º, 11º, and 8º, and sew through the 11º your thread just exited. Continue through the first 8º and 11º just added.
C. Pick up an 8º, and sew through the corresponding 11º on the 12mm rivoli on the other motif.
D. Pick up an 8º, and sew through the 11º and the following 8º added in 17B.
E. Sew through the next 8º in the connector. Pick up an 8º, and sew through the following 8º, 11º, and 8º. Pick up an 11º, and sew through the next 8º.
F. Continue creating and attaching motifs to reach the desired length. For the last motif, finish with step 9.

BACK

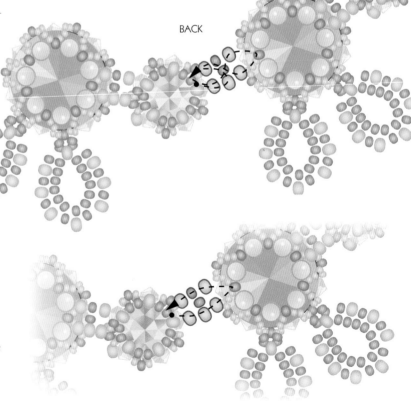

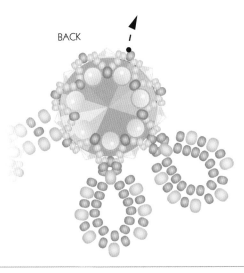

BACK

18 On the last motif, exit the beadwork as shown.

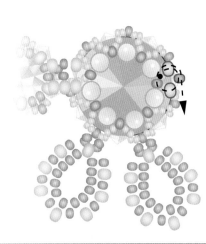

19 Pick up an 8º, 11º, and 8º. Sew through the 11º you first exited. Continue through the next 8º and 11º.

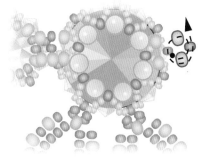

20 Pick up an 8º, 11º, and 8º. Sew through the 11º you first exited. Continue through the three beads just added.

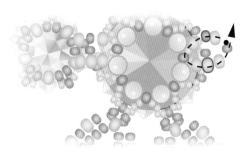

21 A. Pick up an 11º. Sew through the next 8º, 11º, and 8º.
B. Pick up an 8º. Sew through the next 8º and 11º.

22 Repeat steps 19–21 as desired to add an extension. Finish the thread.

23 Attach a new thread about 10 in. (25cm) long. Sew through the beads and exit an end 11º. Pick up an 11º, 8º, 11º, the loop of one half of the clasp, 11º, 8º, and 11º. Sew through the 11º you first exited (from the back). Reinforce the work by sewing through all the beads one more time. Finish the thread, and repeat this step on the other end of the necklace.

Bunnie Earrings

"Trends come and go, and style evolves. It's important to have pieces of jewelry that are time-less and look chic despite ever-changing fashions."
— Karen Elson

1 Thread a needle on a comfortable length of thread, and pick up a 3mm pearl and an 11º seed bead seven times. Close the beads to a circle. Tie a surgeon's knot, and sew through the nearest 11º.

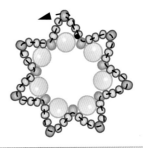

2 Pick up three 15º seed beads, an 11º, and three 15ºs. Sew through the next 11º. Repeat around the ring. Step up through three 15ºs and an 11º.

3 Pick up a 15º, 3mm bicone crystal, and 15º. Sew through the next 11º. Repeat around the ring. Finish by exiting a 3mm bicone crystal.

4 Insert a 14mm rivoli into the bead-work, face-up. Pick up two 11ºs. Sew through the next 3mm bicone crystal. Repeat around the ring. Sew through all the beads once more to reinforce the work. Finish by exiting an outer 11º.

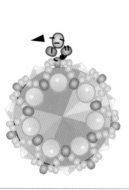

5 Pick up an 11º, 8º seed bead, and 11º. Sew through the 11º you first exited. Continue through the next 11º and the following 8º just added.

6 Pick up 13 11ºs. Sew through the 8º you first exited. Sew through all the beads once more to reinforce the loop. Continue through the next two 11ºs.

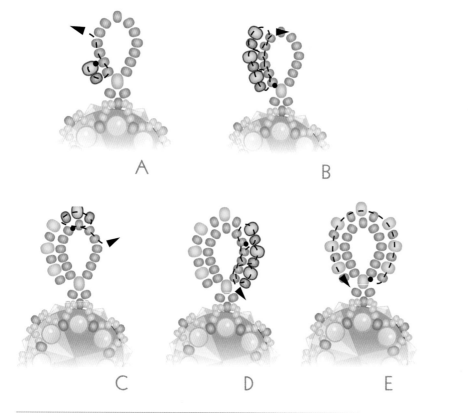

A

B

C

D

E

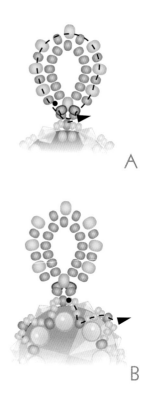

A

B

7 A. Pick up an 8º and an 11º. Sew through two 11ºs. Continue through the next two 11ºs, as shown.
  B. Repeat 7A twice.
  C. Exit the seventh 11º. Pick up an 11º, 8º, and 11º. Sew through the seventh 11º again. Continue through next two 11ºs.
  D. Pick up an 11º and an 8º. Sew through the same two 11ºs. Continue through the next two 11ºs. Repeat twice.
  E. Sew through all the beads you added in steps 7A–D.

8 A. Work on the front side: Pick up an 11º. Sew through the 11º your thread exited at the start of step 5. Pick up another an 11º. Sew through all the beads you added in steps 7A–D (front view).
  B. Continue through the marked beads on the back side. Finish by exiting the marked 11º.

SUPPLIES

- **1g** 15º seed beads
- **1g** 11º seed beads
- **1g** 8º seed beads
- **14** 3mm pearls
- **14** 3mm bicone crystals
- **2** 14mm crystal rivolis
- **1** pair of earring hooks
- Beading needle and thread

"Trends come and go, and style evolves. It's important to have pieces of jewelry that are timeless and look chic despite ever-changing fashions."

— Karen Elson

1 Thread a needle on a comfortable length of thread, and pick up a 3mm pearl and an 11º seed bead seven times. Close the beads to a circle. Tie a surgeon's knot, and sew through the nearest 11º.

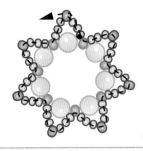

2 Pick up three 15º seed beads, an 11º, and three 15ºs. Sew through the next 11º. Repeat around the ring. Step up through three 15ºs and an 11º.

3 Pick up a 15º, 3mm bicone crystal, and 15º. Sew through the next 11º. Repeat around the ring. Finish by exiting a 3mm bicone crystal.

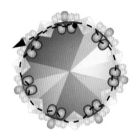

4 Insert a 14mm rivoli into the beadwork, face-up. Pick up two 11ºs. Sew through the next 3mm bicone crystal. Repeat around the ring. Sew through all the beads once more to reinforce the work. Finish by exiting an outer 11º.

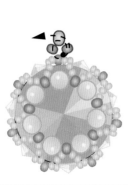

5 Pick up an 11º, 8º seed bead, and 11º. Sew through the 11º you first exited. Continue through the next 11º and the following 8º just added.

6 Pick up 13 11ºs. Sew through the 8º you first exited. Sew through all the beads once more to reinforce the loop. Continue through the next two 11ºs.

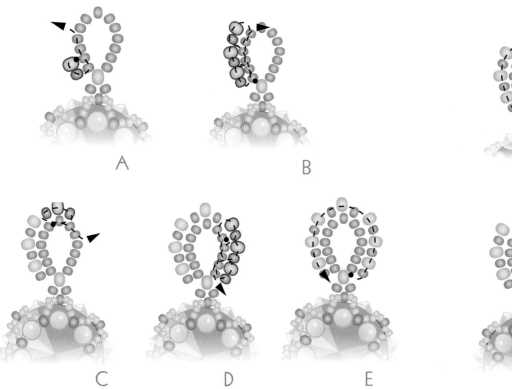

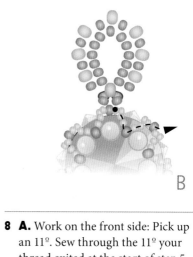

A

B

C

D

E

A

B

7 A. Pick up an 8º and an 11º. Sew through two 11ºs. Continue through the next two 11ºs, as shown.
B. Repeat 7A twice.
C. Exit the seventh 11º. Pick up an 11º, 8º, and 11º. Sew through the seventh 11º again. Continue through next two 11ºs.
D. Pick up an 11º and an 8º. Sew through the same two 11ºs. Continue through the next two 11ºs. Repeat twice.
E. Sew through all the beads you added in steps 7A–D.

8 A. Work on the front side: Pick up an 11º. Sew through the 11º your thread exited at the start of step 5. Pick up another an 11º. Sew through all the beads you added in steps 7A–D (front view).
B. Continue through the marked beads on the back side. Finish by exiting the marked 11º.

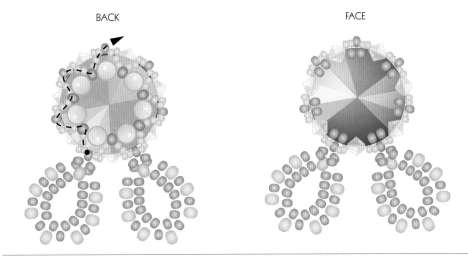

BACK   FACE

9 Repeat step 5–8 to create another "bunny ear." Finish by exiting the marked 11º.

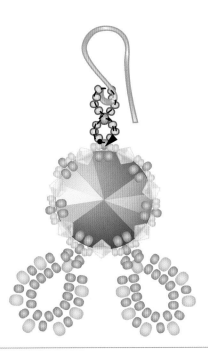

10 Pick up three 15ºs, an 11º, and three 15ºs. Sew through the 11º you first exited, plus three 15ºs and the following 11º. Pick up four 15ºs, an earring hook, and four 15ºs. Sew through the 11º you first exited. Reinforce the work by sewing through all the beads once more. Finish the thread. Repeat to make another earring.

Petra
Necklace

SUPPLIES

 2g 15º seed beads

 4g 11º seed beads

 9g 8º seed beads

 130 GemDuo beads

 130 MiniDuo beads

 70 3mm bicone crystals

20 4mm bicone crystals

32 3.4mm drop beads

50 Arcos par Puca beads

 32 8mm (SS29) set-in stones

1 hook-and-eye or magnetic clasp

Beading needle and thread

"If I had my way, I'd wear jewelry, a great pair of heels, and nothing else."

—Jada Pinkett Smith

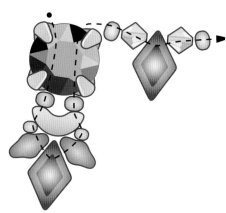

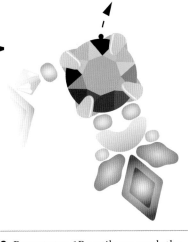

1 A. Thread a needle on a comfortable length of thread.
B. Pick up an 8mm set-in stone, an 8º seed bead, an Arcos bead, an 11º seed bead, a MiniDuo bead, a GemDuo bead, a MiniDuo, and an 11º. Sew through the third hole of the Arcos. (Make sure the GemDuos are facing up!) Pick up an 8º. Sew through the free hole of the set-in stone.
C. Pick up an 8º, 3mm bicone crystal, GemDuo, 3mm bicone crystal, and 8º.

2 Repeat step 1B until you reach the desired length. Finish by exiting the free hole of the last 8mm set-in stone.

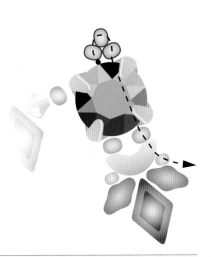

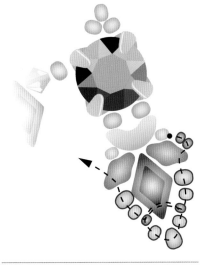

3 Pick up three 8ºs. Sew back through the second hole of the 8mm set-in stone, the 8º, the Arcos, and the following 11º.

4 A. Pick up two 15ºs. Sew through the free hole of the MiniDuo.
B. Pick up an 8º, 11º, and 15º. Sew through the free hole of the GemDuo.
C. Pick up a 15º, 11º, 3.4mm drop bead, and 11º. Sew through the 15º, the GemDuo, and the first 15º you just added at the start of this stitch.
D. Pick up an 11º and an 8º. Sew through the free hole of the nearest-MiniDuo.

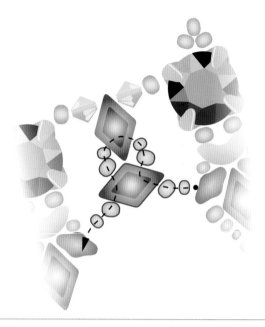

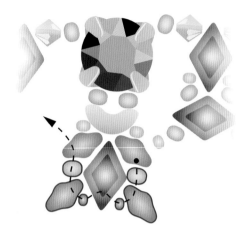

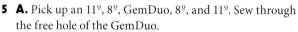

5 **A.** Pick up an 11º, 8º, GemDuo, 8º, and 11º. Sew through the free hole of the GemDuo.
B. Pick up an 11º and an 8º. Sew through the free hole of the GemDuo.
C. Pick up an 8º and an 11º. Sew through the free hole of the nearest MiniDuo. Repeat steps 4B–5C five times.

6 Pick up an 8º, MiniDuo, and 15º. Sew through the free hole of the GemDuo. Pick up a 15º, MiniDuo, and 8º. Sew through the free hole of the next MiniDuo.

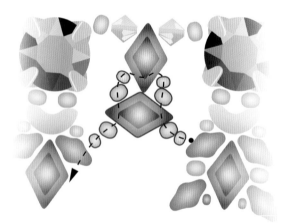

7 **A.** Pick up an 11º, 8º, GemDuo, 8º, and 11º. Sew through the free hole of the GemDuo.
B. Pick up an 11º and an 8º. Sew through the free hole of the GemDuo.
C. Pick up an 8º and an 11º. Sew through the free hole of the MiniDuo.

8 Repeat steps 6–7 until you reach the last five repeats, ending and adding thread as needed.

9 Repeat steps 4B–5C five times. Repeat steps 4B–4D, exiting the last MiniDuo.

Color
Option

10 Pick up two 15ºs. Sew through the next 11º, Arcos, 8º, and 8mm set-in stone.

11 Pick up three 8ºs. Sew back through the set-in stone, and finish the thread.

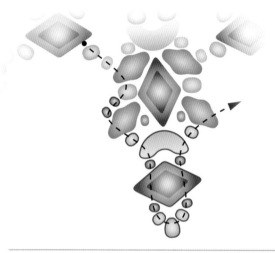

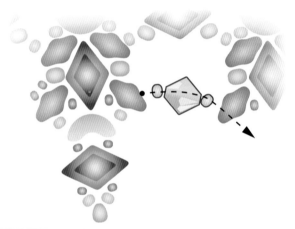

12 A. Attach a new thread. Exit a GemDuo, as shown, and sew through the marked beads.
 B. Pick up two 15ºs. Sew through the free hole of the MiniDuo.
 C. Pick up an 11º, Arcos, 15º, GemDuo, 15º, 11º, drop, 11º, and a 15º. Sew back through the free hole of the GemDuo.
 D. Pick up a 15º. Sew through the free hole of the Arcos.
 E. Pick up an 11º. Sew through the free hole of the next MiniDuo.

13 Pick up an 11º, 4mm bicone crystal, and 11º. Sew through the free hole of the next MiniDuo.

14 Repeat steps 12B–13 to the end of the necklace. Finish with step 12A, and finish the thread.

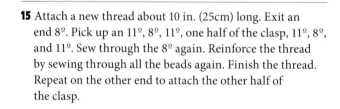

15 Attach a new thread about 10 in. (25cm) long. Exit an end 8º. Pick up an 11º, 8º, 11º, one half of the clasp, 11º, 8º, and 11º. Sew through the 8º again. Reinforce the thread by sewing through all the beads again. Finish the thread. Repeat on the other end to attach the other half of the clasp.

Chrysta
Pendant

SUPPLIES

- .5g 15º seed beads
- 1g 11º seed beads
- **10** 8º seed beads
- **12** MiniDuo beads
- **24** 6x8mm tulip petal beads
- **1** 10mm (SS47) crystal rivoli
- Beading needle and thread

"I like for jewelry to tell a story about what I'm wearing. That's more important to me than a name, brand, or label."

— Nikki Reed

1 Thread a needle on a comfortable length of thread. Pick up a tulip petal bead and an 11º seed bead six times. Sew through the first petal again. Knot the threads twice. Then, sew through the next petal.

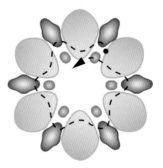

2 Pick up a MiniDuo bead. Sew through the next petal. Repeat to complete the round and exit the next 11º.

3 Work on the front side: Pick up two 15º seed beads, an 11º, and two 15ºs. Sew through the next 11º. Repeat around the ring. Step up through two 15ºs and an 11º.

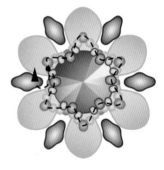

4 Place a 10mm crystal rivoli in the beadwork, face up. Pick up a 15º, 11º, and 15º. Sew through the next 11º. Repeat around the ring.

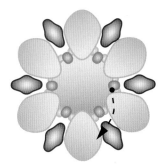

5 Exit an 11º between petals (back side). Continue through the next petal and the following MiniDuo as shown.

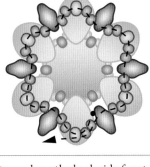

6 Continue to work on the back side for steps 6–8. Pick up two 11ºs, an 8º seed bead, and two 11ºs. Sew through the next MiniDuo (not through the free holes). Step up through two 11ºs and the following 8º.

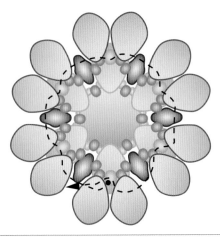

7 A. Pick up a petal. Sew through the free hole of the next MiniDuo.
   B. Pick up a petal. Sew through the next 8º.
   C. Repeat steps A and B around the ring. Finish by exiting the marked petal.

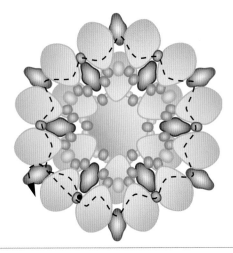

8 A. Pick up an 11º. Sew through the next petal.
   B. Pick up a MiniDuo. Sew through the following petal. Repeat around the ring. Finish by exiting the first MiniDuo added. Sew back through the free hole of the same MiniDuo (changing work direction).

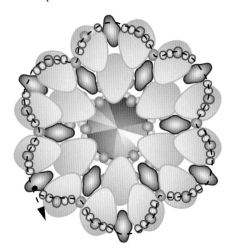

9 A. Work on the front side: Pick up two 15ºs, an 11º, and two 15ºs. Sew through the next 11º.
   B. Pick up two 15ºs, an 11º, and two 15ºs. Sew through the free hole of the next MiniDuo. Repeat around the ring. Finish by exiting the MiniDuo you first exited.

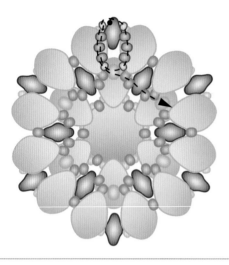

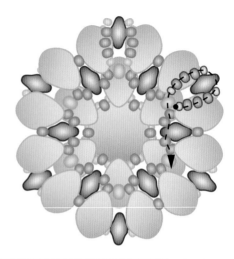

10 A. Work on the back side: Pick up a 15º, three 11ºs, and a 15º. Sew through the marked 8º.

B. Pick up a 15º, three 11ºs, and a 15º. Sew through the MiniDuo. Continue through the marked beads to the next 8º.

11 A. Pick up a 15º, three 11ºs, and a 15º. Sew through the next MiniDuo.

B. Pick up a 15º, three 11ºs, and a 15º. Sew through the 8º. Continue through the marked beads to the next 8º.

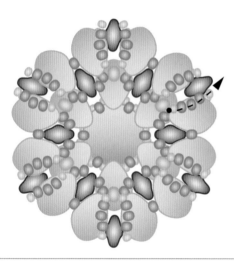

12 Repeat step 11 around. Step up through the first 15º, three 11ºs, and a 15º.

13 Make a hanging loop (optional): Pick up three 11ºs, four 15ºs, and three 11ºs. Sew through the adjacent 15º and MiniDuo. Reinforce the loop by sewing through all the beads again. Finish the thread.

SUPPLIES

- ⬤ **1g** 15º seed beads
- ⬤ **4g** 11º seed beads
- ⬤ **4g** 8º seed beads
- **42** ZoliDuo beads, right version
- **42** ZoliDuo beads, left version
- ◇ **60** 3mm bicone crystals
- ◇ **25** 4mm bicone crystals
- ◇ **150** Silky beads
- ▯ **18** O-Beads
- ○ **50** 4mm pearls
- ⬤ **24** 8mm pearls
- ⬤ **25** 6x9mm top-drilled drop beads
- **1** clasp
- Beading needle and thread

"Make the most of yourself by fanning the tiny, inner sparks of possibility into flames of achievement."

— Golda Meir

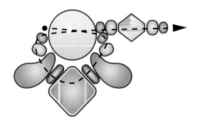

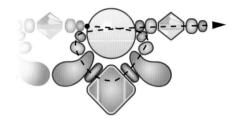

1 A. Thread a needle on a comfortable length of thread, and pick up an 8mm pearl, 11º seed bead, 8º seed bead, ZoliDuo bead (left, concave side), O-Bead, Silky bead, O-Bead, ZoliDuo bead (right, convex side), 8º, and 11º. (Make sure the ZoliDuos and Silky are facing up!) Sew through the 8mm pearl again in the same direction.
B. Pick up an 11º, 8º, 4mm bicone crystal, 8º, and 11º.

2 Repeat steps 1A–1B until you reach the desired length.

3 Finish at step 1A.

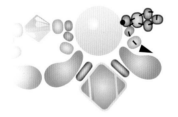

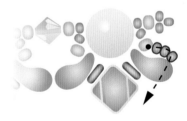

4 Pick up an 11º, an 8º, and three 11ºs. Sew back through the 8º and 11º, and the following 11º and 8º.

5 Pick up three 11ºs. Sew through the free hole of the adjacent ZoliDuo.

36

Color
Option

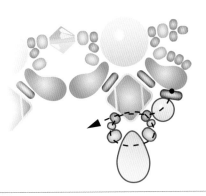

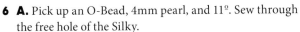

6 A. Pick up an O-Bead, 4mm pearl, and 11º. Sew through the free hole of the Silky.
B. Pick up an 11º, 15º seed bead, 8º, top-drilled drop, 8º, and 15º. Sew through the 11º, Silky, and 11º.

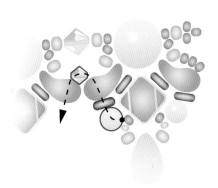

7 A. Pick up a 4mm pearl and an O-Bead. Sew through the free hole of the adjacent ZoliDuo.
B. Pick up a 3mm bicone crystal. Sew through the free hole of the next ZoliDuo.

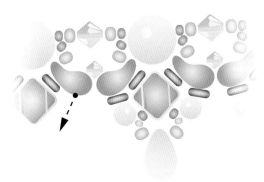

8 Repeat steps 6–7 three times, ending and adding thread as needed.

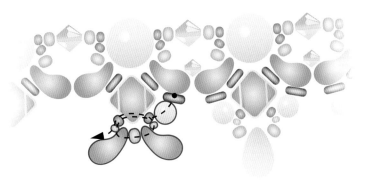

9 A. Pick up an O-Bead, 4mm pearl, and 11º, and sew through the free hole of the next Silky.
B. Pick up an 11º, 15º, ZoliDuo (right), 8º, ZoliDuo (left), and 15º. Sew through the adjacent 11º, Silky, 11º, and 15º.

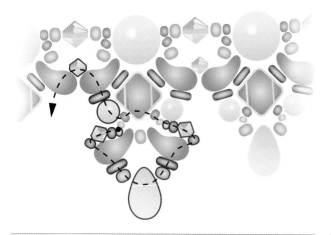

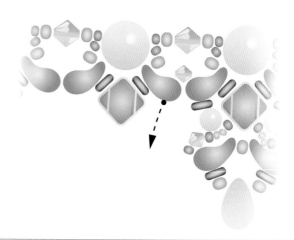

10 A. Pick up a 15º, 11º, 3mm bicone crystal, and 11º. Sew through the free hole of the adjacent ZoliDuo.
B. Pick up an O-Bead, 8º, top-drilled drop, 8º, and O-Bead. Sew through the free hole of the next ZoliDuo.
C. Pick up an 11º, 3mm bicone crystal, 11º, and 15º. Sew through the next 15º, 11º, Silky, and 11º.
D. Pick up a 4mm pearl and an O-Bead. Sew through the free hole of the next ZoliDuo.
E. Pick up a 3mm bicone crystal. Sew through the free hole of the next ZoliDuo.

11 Repeat steps 9–10 up to the last four pairs of Silkys.

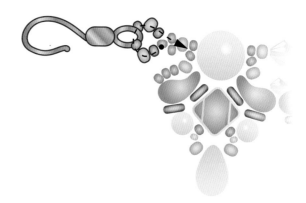

12 Repeat steps 6–7 over the remaining Silkys. Finish at step 7A. Pick up three 11ºs. Sew through the end 8º and the following 11º. Pick up an 11º, an 8º, and three 11ºs. Sew back through the 8º and the 11º, and continue through the 8mm pearl. Finish the thread.

13 Attach a new thread about 10 in. (25cm) long. Exit the end 11º. Pick up an 11º, 8º, 11º, one half of the clasp, 11º, 8º, and 11º. Sew through the same 11º, closing the beads to a circle. Reinforce the thread by sewing through all the beads again. Finish the thread. Repeat on the other side to attach the other half of the clasp.

Offelia Bracelet

SUPPLIES

- **2g** 11º seed beads
- **2g** 8º seed beads
- **18** ZoliDuo beads, right version
- **18** ZoliDuo beads, left version
- **8** 4mm bicone crystals
- **18** Silky beads
- **72** O-Beads
- **36** 4mm pearls
- **9** 8mm pearls

Magnetic clasp

Beading needle and thread

> "It took me quite a long time to develop a voice, and now that I have it, I am not going to be silent."
>
> — Madeleine Albright

Color Option

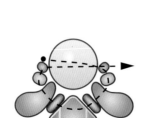

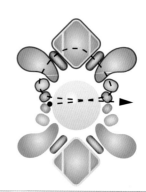

1 Thread a needle on a comfortable length of thread, and pick up an 8mm pearl, 11º seed bead, 8º seed bead, ZoliDuo bead (left, concave side), O-Bead, Silky bead, O-Bead, ZoliDuo bead (right, convex side), 8º, and 11º. (Make sure the Zoli-Duos and Silky are facing up!) Sew through the 8mm pearl again.

2 Pick up an 11º, 8º, ZoliDuo (right, concave side), O-Bead, Silky, O-Bead, ZoliDuo (left, convex side), 8º, and 11º. (Make sure the ZoliDuos and Silky are facing up!) Sew through the 8mm pearl.

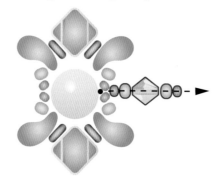

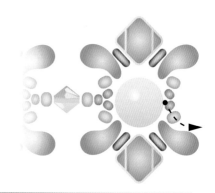

3 Pick up an 11º, 8º, 4mm bicone crystal, 8º, and 11º.

4 Repeat steps 1–3 until you reach the desired length. Finish at step 2, and sew through the marked 11º and 8º.

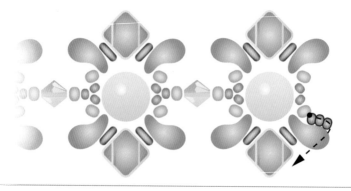

5 Pick up three 11ºs. Sew through the free hole of the nearest ZoliDuo.

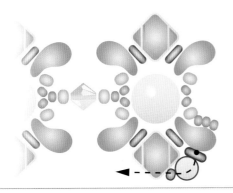

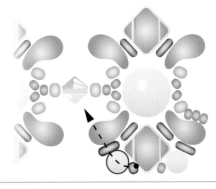

6 Pick up an O-Bead, 4mm pearl, and 11º. Sew through the free hole of the next Silky.

7 Pick up an 11º, 4mm pearl, and O-Bead. Sew through the free hole of the next ZoliDuo.

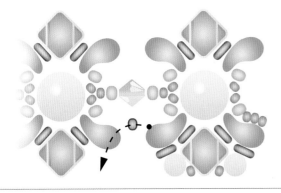

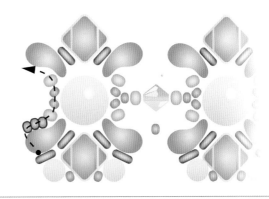

8 Pick up an 11º. Sew through the free hole of the next ZoliDuo.

9 Repeat steps 6–8 for the length of the bracelet, ending and adding thread as needed. Finish at step 7. Pick up three 11ºs. Sew through the marked beads.

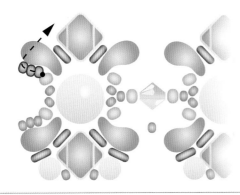

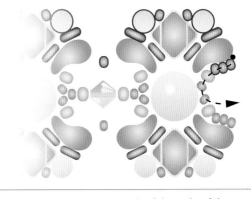

10 Pick up three 11ºs. Sew through the free hole of the next ZoliDuo.

11 Repeat steps 6–8 for the length of this side of the bracelet. Finish at step 7. Pick up three 11ºs. Sew through the marked beads. Finish the thread.

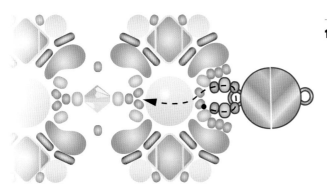

12 Attach a new thread about 10 in. (25cm) long. Exit the end pair of 11ºs. Pick up an 11º, 8º, 11º, one half of the clasp, 11º, 8º, and 11º. Sew through the marked 11º to close the beads to a circle. Reinforce the clasp connection by sewing through the loop of beads again. Finish the thread. Repeat on the other side to attach the other half of the clasp.

Offelia
Earrings

SUPPLIES

- **20** 15º seed beads
- **50** 11º seed beads
- **20** 8º seed beads
- **4** ZoliDuo beads, right version
- **4** ZoliDuo beads, left version
- **8** 3mm bicone crystals
- **2** Silky beads
- **12** O-Beads
- **2** 8mm pearls
- **4** 4mm pearls
- **2** 6x9mm top-drilled drop beads
- Pair of earring hooks
- Beading needle and thread

"Trust yourself. Create the kind of self that you will be happy to live with all your life."

— Golda Meir

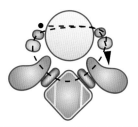

1 Thread a needle on a comfortable length of thread. Pick up an 8mm pearl, 11º seed bead, 8º seed bead, ZoliDuo bead (left), O-Bead, Silky bead, O-Bead, ZoliDuo bead (right), 8º, and 11º. (Make sure the ZoliDuos are facing up!) Sew through the 8mm pearl again. Continue through the following 11º and 8º.

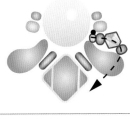

2 Pick up a 15º seed bead, 11º, 3mm bicone crystal, and 11º. Sew through the free hole of the adjacent ZoliDuo.

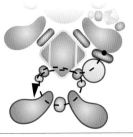

3 A. Pick up an O-Bead, 4mm pearl, and 11º. Sew through the free hole of the Silky.
B. Pick up an 11º, 15º, ZoliDuo (right), 8º, ZoliDuo (left), and 15º. Sew through the 11º, Silky, 11º, and the following 15º.

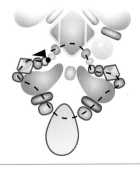

4 A. Pick up a 15º, 11º, 3mm bicone crystal, and 11º. Sew through the free hole of the adjacent ZoliDuo.
B. Pick up an O-Bead, 8º, top-drilled drop, 8º, and O-Bead. Sew through the free hole of the next ZoliDuo.
C. Pick up an 11º, 3mm bicone crystal, 11º, and 15º. Sew through the next 15º, 11º, Silky, and 11º.

5 A. Pick up a 4mm pearl and an O-Bead, and sew through the free hole of the next ZoliDuo.
B. Pick up an 11º, 3mm bicone crystal, 11º, and 15º. Sew through the nearest 8º, 11º, and 8mm pearl.

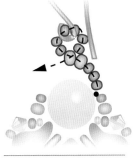

6 Pick up three 11ºs, two 8ºs, three 11ºs, an earring hook, and three 11ºs. Sew through the second 8º of the pair of 8ºs just picked up.

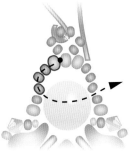

7 Pick up an 8º and three 11ºs. Sew through the 8mm pearl. Reinforce the loop by sewing through all the beads again. Finish the thread. Repeat to make a second earring.

Yarden
Necklace

SUPPLIES

- **1.5g** 15º seed beads
- **7g** 11º seed beads
- **11g** 8º seed beads
- **80** 3mm bicone crystals
- **34** SuperDuo beads
- **100** 3mm pearls
- **52** GemDuo beads
- **12** 8mm (SS39) chatons
- **17** 6mm rose montées
- Magnetic clasp
- Beading needle and thread

*"I choose to make the
rest of my life the best
of my life."*

— Louise Hay

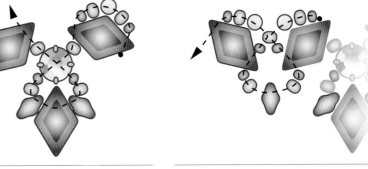

1 A. Thread a needle on a comfortable length of thread, and pick up a GemDuo bead, 11º seed bead, 8º seed bead, 3mm pearl, 8º, and 11º. (Make sure the GemDuos are facing up!) Sew through the free hole of the GemDuo.
B. Pick up an 8º, rose montée, 11º, 8º, SuperDuo bead, GemDuo, SuperDuo, 8º, and 11º. Cross through the rose montée so the face is face-up.
C. Pick up an 8º and a GemDuo.

2 A. Pick up an 11º, 8º, 3mm pearl, 8º, and 11º. Sew through the free hole of the same GemDuo.
B. Pick up an 11º, 8º, SuperDuo, 8º, 11º, GemDuo, and 11º. Sew through the second 8º added in the previous stitch. (Make sure the GemDuos are facing up!)
C. Pick up a 3mm pearl, 8º, and 11º. Sew through the free hole of the same GemDuo.

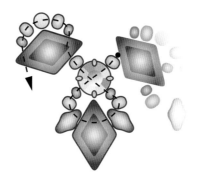

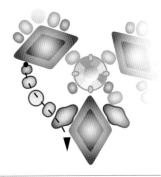

3 Repeat 1B–2C until you reach your desired necklace length, ending and adding thread as needed.

4 Pick up an 11º, 8º, 3mm pearl, and 8º. Sew through the free hole of the SuperDuo.

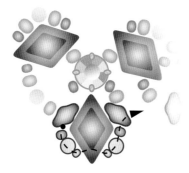

5 A. Pick up an 11º, 3mm pearl, and 15º seed bead. Sew through the free hole of the same GemDuo.
B. Pick up a 15º, 3mm pearl, and 11º. Sew through the free hole of the nearest SuperDuo.

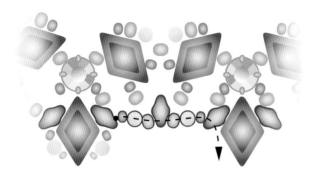

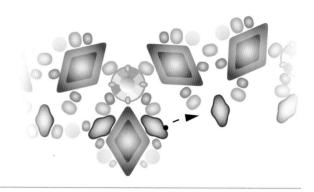

6 A. Pick up an 11º, 3mm pearl and 8º. Sew through the free hole of the next SuperDuo.
B. Pick up an 8º, 3mm pearl, and 11º. Sew through the free hole of the next SuperDuo.

7 Repeat steps 5, 6, 5, 6, and 5.

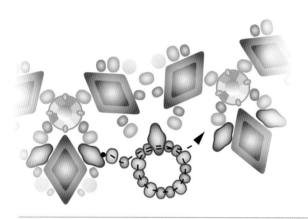

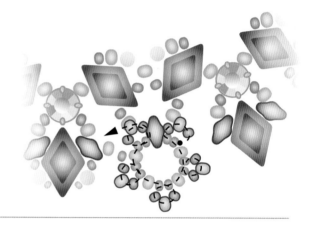

8 A. Pick up an 8º and three 11ºs. Sew through the free hole of the next SuperDuo.
B. Pick up two 11ºs and an 8º four times. Sew through the second and the third 11º you added in step 8A. Continue through the next SuperDuo and the following two 11ºs.

9 Pick up an 11º, 8º, and 11º. Sew through the same two 11ºs. Then sew through the following 8º and two 11ºs. Repeat around. After the last beads are added, step up through the 8º (changing work direction).

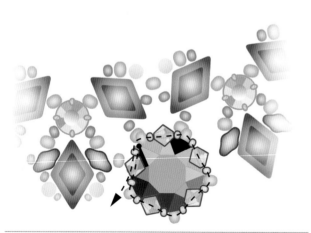

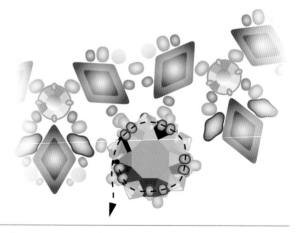

10 Place an 8mm round stone in the beadwork, face up. Pick up a 15º, 3mm bicone crystal, and 15º. Sew through the next 8º. Repeat around. Finish by exiting the marked 3mm crystal.

11 Pick up two 11ºs, and sew through the next 3mm crystal. Repeat around. Continue through the following 15º and 8º.

BACK

FRONT

12 A. Sew through the back side of the beadwork, passing through the marked beads.

B. Pick up an 11º and an 8º. Sew through the free hole of the adjacent SuperDuo.

C. Repeat steps 5 and 8–12B until there are three downward-pointing GemDuos remaining.

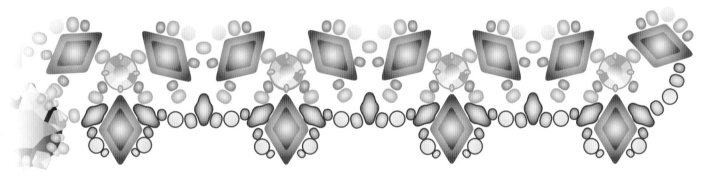

13 Repeat steps 5, 6, 5, 6, and 5 over the remaining length of the necklace. At the end, pick up an 8º, 3mm pearl, 8º, and 11º, sew through the last GemDuo, and end the thread.

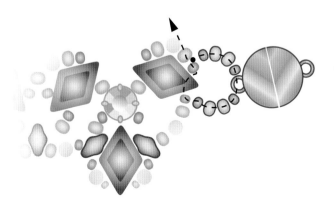

14 Attach a new thread about 10 in. (25cm) long, and sew through the beadwork to exit the 11º on top of the last GemDuo. Pick up an 11º, two 8ºs, 11º, one half of the clasp, 11º, two 8ºs, and an 11º. Close to a circle on the same 11º you exited at the beginning of this step. Sew through all the beads again to reinforce the thread. Finish the thread. Repeat on the other side of the necklace to finish.

Victory Bracelet

SUPPLIES

- **7g** 15º seed beads
- **9g** 11º seed beads
- **160** SuperDuo beads
- **162** 3mm bicone crystals
- **18** 8mm (SS39) chatons, **9** of each color
- **10** 5x10mm navettes
- **20** AVA beads

Magnetic clasp

Beading needle and thread

"Be proud of yourself; remember that people can only go where you have already been— they have no idea where you are going next."

— Liz Lange

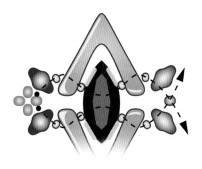

1 Thread a needle on a comfortable length of thread and pick up four 11º seed beads. Sew through the first 11º again. Center the beads on the thread, and thread a needle on the tail.

2 A. On one thread, pick up a SuperDuo bead, 15º seed bead, AVA bead, 15º, 5x10mm navette, and 15º. Sew through the other arm of the AVA, as shown. Pick up a 15º and a SuperDuo.
B. On the other thread, pick up a SuperDuo, 15º, AVA, and 15º. Sew through the free hole of the existing navette. Pick up a 15º, and sew through the other arm of the AVA. Pick up a 15º and a SuperDuo.
C. Cross both threads through an 11º, as shown.

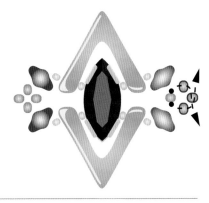

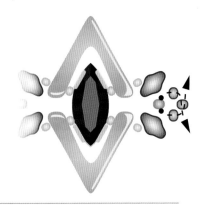

3 Pick up an 11º on each thread. Cross both threads through another 11º, as shown.

4 Repeat steps 2 and 3 until you reach the desired length. Finish with step 3.

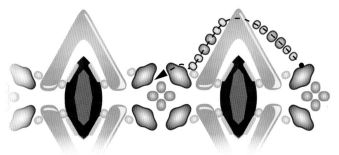

5 With one thread, sew through the next 11º and the free hole of the end SuperDuo.
A. Pick up two 15ºs, two 11ºs, and two 15ºs. Sew through the free hole of the next AVA.
B. Pick up two 15ºs, two 11ºs, and two 15ºs. Sew through the free hole of the nearest SuperDuo.

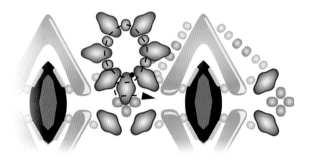

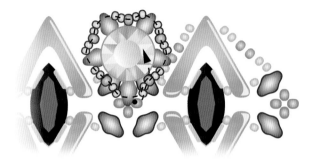

6 A. Pick up a SuperDuo. Sew through the free hole of the next SuperDuo.

B. Pick up an 11º and a SuperDuo four times. Then pick up an 11º. Close the beads to a circle on the same Super-Duo where you began this step.

C. Continue through the first SuperDuo you added in step 6A. Sew back through the free hole of the same SuperDuo (changing work direction).

7 Pick up two 15ºs, an 11º, and two 15ºs. Skip the adjacent SuperDuo. Sew through the free hole of the following SuperDuo. Pick up two 15ºs, an 11º, and two 15ºs, and sew through the free hole of the next SuperDuo. Repeat this last stitch two more times. Then pick up two 15ºs, an 11º, and two 15ºs. Skip the next SuperDuo, and sew through the next SuperDuo. Step up through the first two 15ºs and one 11º you added. Place an 8mm chaton face up in the beadwork.

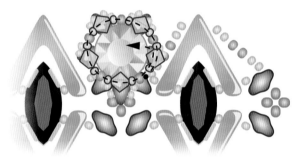

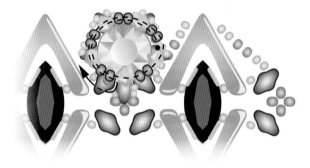

8 Pick up a 15º, 3mm bicone crystal, and 15º. Sew through the next 11º. Repeat around. Finish by exiting a 3mm bicone crystal.

9 Pick up two 11ºs. Sew through the next 3mm bicone crystal. Repeat around. Reinforce the work by sewing through all the beads again. Finish by exiting two 15ºs, and sew down through the lower 15º into the SuperDuo, as shown. Your needle will be pointing toward the opposite end of the bracelet.

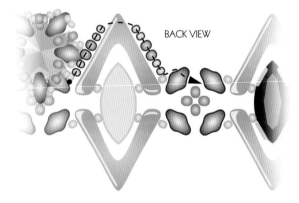

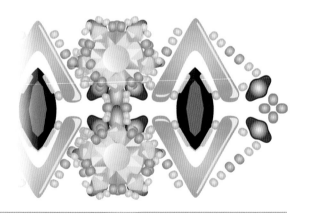

10 Repeat from step 5 for the length of the bracelet (back view).

11 Repeat steps 5–10 along the other edge of the bracelet with the remaining thread.

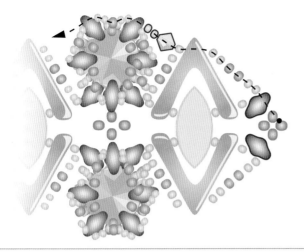

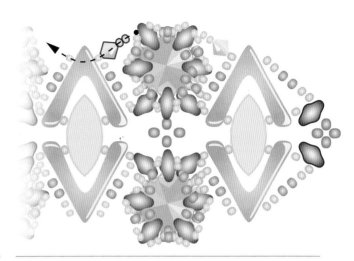

12 Exit the first 15º after the end AVA. Pick up a 3mm bicone crystal and two 15ºs. Sew through the marked SuperDuo, two 15ºs, 11º, two 15ºs, and SuperDuo.

13 Pick up two 15ºs and a 3mm bicone crystal. Sew through the marked 15º, the AVA, and a 15º.

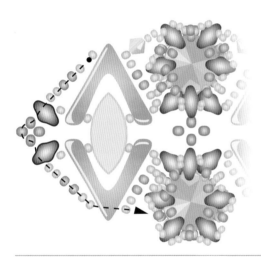

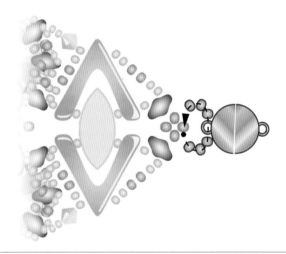

14 Repeat steps 12–13 for the length of the bracelet. At the end, sew through the marked beads to the other side. Repeat steps 12–13 along the other edge. Finish the threads.

15 Attach a new thread about 10 in. (25cm) long. Exit the center 11º at the end. Pick up three 11ºs, half of the clasp, and three 11ºs. Close the beads to a circle on the same 11º you began this step. Sew through all the beads again to reinforce. Finish the thread. Repeat on the other side of the bracelet to attach the other half of the clasp.

Color Option

SUPPLIES

 2g 11º seed beads

 4g 8º seed beads

 22 Arcos par Puca beads

 68 4mm bicone crystals

 22 5x10mm navettes

 44 Vexolo beads

Magnetic clasp

Beading needle and thread

1 Thread a needle on a comfortable length of thread, and pick up an Arcos bead, 11º seed bead, two Vexolo beads, 8º seed bead, 5x10mm navette, and 11º. Sew through the third hole of the Arcos, as shown.

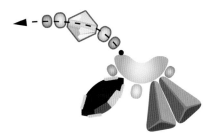

2 Pick up an 11º, 8º, 4mm bicone crystal, 8º, and 11º.

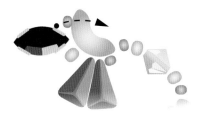

3 Repeat steps 1–2 until you reach the desired length. Finish with step 1.

4 Pick up an 11º, two 8ºs, and 11º. Sew through the free hole of the last navette you added.

Color
Option

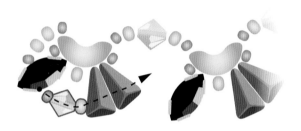

5 Pick up an 11º, 4mm bicone crystal, and 8º. Sew through the free hole of both Vexolos.

6 Pick up an 11º, 4mm bicone crystal, and 8º. Sew through the free hole of the next navette. Repeat steps 5–6 to the end of the necklace.

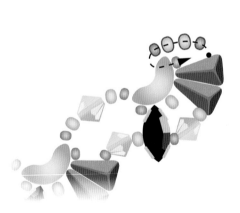

7 At the end, pick up an 11º, two 8ºs, and 11º. Sew from the top through the Arcos and the adjacent 11º. Finish the threads.

8 Attach a new thread about 10 in. (25cm) long, and sew through the beads to exit two 8ºs. Pick up an 11º, 8º, 11º, half of the clasp, 11º, 8º, and 11º. Sew back through the same two 8ºs you first exited. Reinforce the work by sewing through all the beads again. Finish the thread. Repeat on the other side of the necklace to attach the other half of the clasp.

Fani
Bracelet

- **1g** 11º seed beads
- **2g** 8º seed beads
- **46** 3mm bicone crystals
- **39** GemDuo beads
- **80** Vexolo beads
- **8** 7x15mm navettes

3-loop box clasp

Beading needle and thread

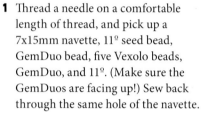

1 Thread a needle on a comfortable length of thread, and pick up a 7x15mm navette, 11º seed bead, GemDuo bead, five Vexolo beads, GemDuo, and 11º. (Make sure the GemDuos are facing up!) Sew back through the same hole of the navette.

2 Pick up an 11º, 8º seed bead, and 11º. Sew through the other hole of the navette, as shown.

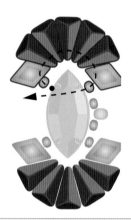
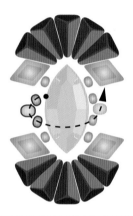

3 Pick up an 11º, GemDuo, five Vexolos, GemDuo, and 11º. Sew back through the navette again.

4 Pick up an 11º, 8º, and 11º. Sew through the opposite hole of the navette. Continue through the 11º and the following 8º, as shown.

"People will stare. Make it worth their while."

— Harry Winston

Color Option

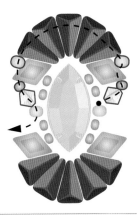

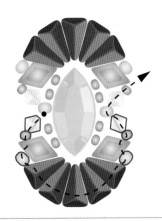

5 Pick up a 3mm bicone crystal and an 11º. Sew through the free hole of the adjacent GemDuo. Pick up an 8º. Sew through the outer hole of all five Vexolos. Pick up an 8º. Sew through the free hole of the next GemDuo. Pick up an 11º and a 3mm bicone crystal. Sew through the next 8º.

6 Repeat step 5 on the other side. Finish by exiting a 3mm bicone crystal and 11º, as shown.

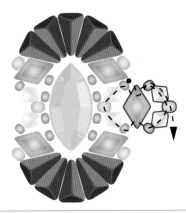

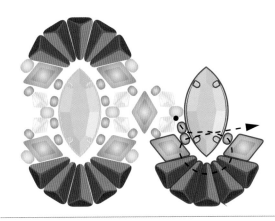

7 Pick up a GemDuo, 11º, 3mm bicone crystal, 8º, 3mm bicone crystal, and 11º. Sew through the free hole of the GemDuo you just added. Continue through the marked beads. Finish by exiting the 8º you added in this step.

8 Pick up an 11º, navette, 11º, GemDuo, five Vexolos, GemDuo, and 11º. Sew through the same hole of the navette.

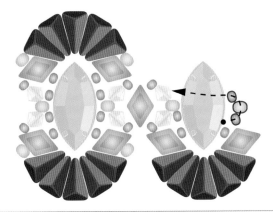

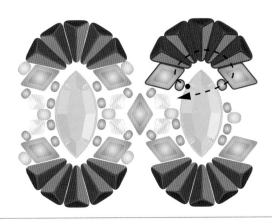

9 Pick up an 11º, 8º, and 11º. Sew through the other holes on the navette as shown.

10 Pick up an 11º, GemDuo, five Vexolos, GemDuo, and 11º. Sew through the same hole of the navette.

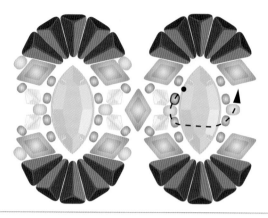

11 Pick up an 11º. Sew through the marked beads. Finish by exiting an 8º, as shown.

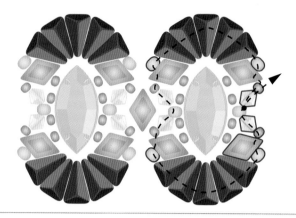

12 Pick up a 3mm bicone crystal and an 11º. Sew through the GemDuo. Pick up an 8º. Sew through all five Vexolos. Pick up an 8º. Sew through the GemDuo. Continue through the marked beads. Finish by exiting the next five Vexolos. Pick up an 8º. Sew through the GemDuo. Pick up an 11º and a 3mm bicone crystal. Sew through the 8º where you began this step. Continue through the marked 3mm bicone crystal and the following 11º.

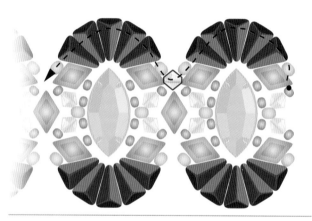

13 A. Repeat steps 7–12 to the desired length or until you have eight motifs.
B. After adding the final motif, sew through the beads, exiting the 8º after the five Vexolos. Pick up a 3mm bicone crystal. Sew through the next 8º, five Vexolos, and the following 8º. Repeat over both sides. End the threads.

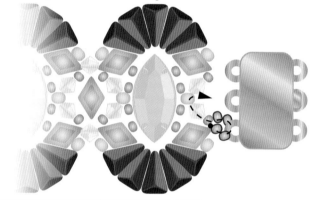

14 Attach a new thread about 10 in. (25cm) long. Exit the 11º after a 3mm bicone crystal. Pick up two 11ºs, the first loop of the clasp, and two 11ºs. Sew back through the 11º you first exited. Sew through all the beads again to reinforce, and sew through the beads to the center 8º.

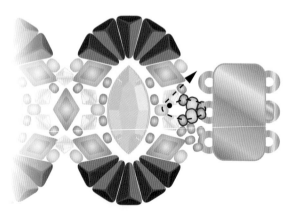

15 Pick up an 11º, 8º, and 11º. Sew through the middle loop on the clasp. Pick up an 11º, 8º, and 11º, and sew back through the 11º you first exited. Sew through all the beads again to reinforce. Sew through the beads to the 11º after the next 3mm bicone crystal.

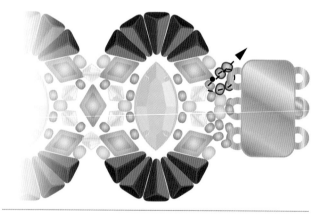

16 Pick up two 11ºs, the third loop of the clasp, and two 11ºs. Sew back through the 11º you first exited. Sew through all the beads again to reinforce. Finish the thread.

17 Repeat steps 14–16 on the other end of the bracelet to attach the other half of the clasp.

Vicki
Necklace

SUPPLIES

 **2g** 15º seed beads

 **7g** 11º seed beads

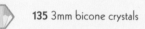 **11g** 8º seed beads

 **140** GemDuo beads

 **24** MiniDuo beads

135 3mm bicone crystals

140 O-Beads

12 6x9mm top-drilled drop beads

12 14mm crystal rivolis

Hook-and-eye clasp

Beading thread and needle

"Iconic and unforgettable jewelry is made with simple inspiration and high-quality materials."

— Isabella

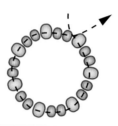

1 Thread a needle on a comfortable length of thread. Pick up an 8º seed bead and two 11º seed beads a total of seven times. Sew through all the beads again, and knot twice.

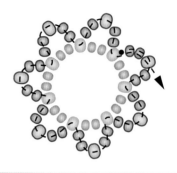

2 A. Sew through the nearest 8º. Pick up two 11ºs, an 8º, and two 11ºs, and sew through the next 8º. Repeat around the ring.
B. At the end, step up through two 11ºs and the following 8º.

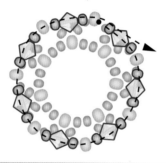

3 Pick up an 11º, 3mm crystal, and 11º. Sew through the next 8º. Repeat around the ring. Finish by exiting the first 3mm crystal you added.

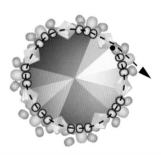

4 A. Place a 14mm rivoli in the beadwork, face up. Pick up three 15º seed beads. Sew through the next 3mm crystal. Repeat around the ring.
B. At the end, step up through the adjacent 11º and following 8º added in step 2A.

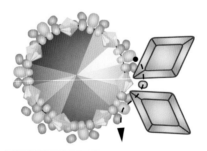

5 Pick up a GemDuo bead, a 15º, and a GemDuo. Sew through the next 8º. (Make sure the GemDuos are facing up!)

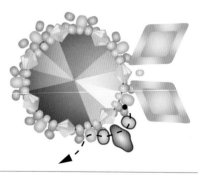

6 Pick up an 8º, MiniDuo, and 8º. Sew through the next 8º.

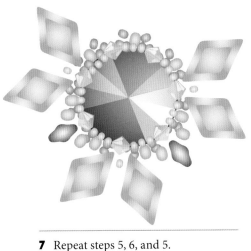

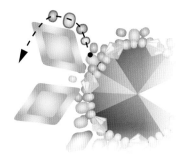

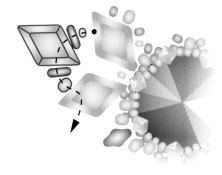

7 Repeat steps 5, 6, and 5.

8 Pick up a 15º, 11º, 8º, and 11º. Sew through the free hole of the last GemDuo to change direction.

9 Pick up a 15º, O-Bead, GemDuo, O-Bead, and 8º. (Make sure the GemDuos are facing up!). Sew through the free hole of the next GemDuo.

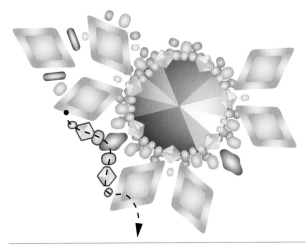

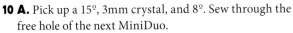

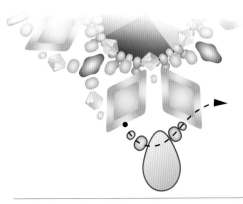

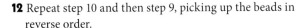

10 A. Pick up a 15º, 3mm crystal, and 8º. Sew through the free hole of the next MiniDuo.
B. Pick up an 8º, 3mm crystal, and 15º. Sew through the free hole of the next GemDuo.

11 Pick up a 15º, 8º, 6x9mm drop bead, 8º, and 15º. Sew through the free hole of the next GemDuo.

12 Repeat step 10 and then step 9, picking up the beads in reverse order.

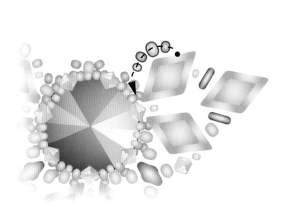

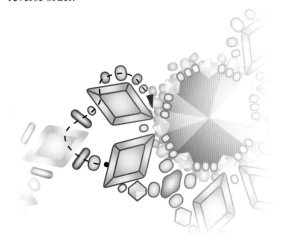

13 Pick up an 11º, 8º, 11º, and 15º. Sew through the marked 8º. End the thread.

14 Create a new motif following steps 1–8. In step 9, connect to the GemDuo from the previous motif. Continue following steps 10–13. Create as many motifs as needed (approximately 11).

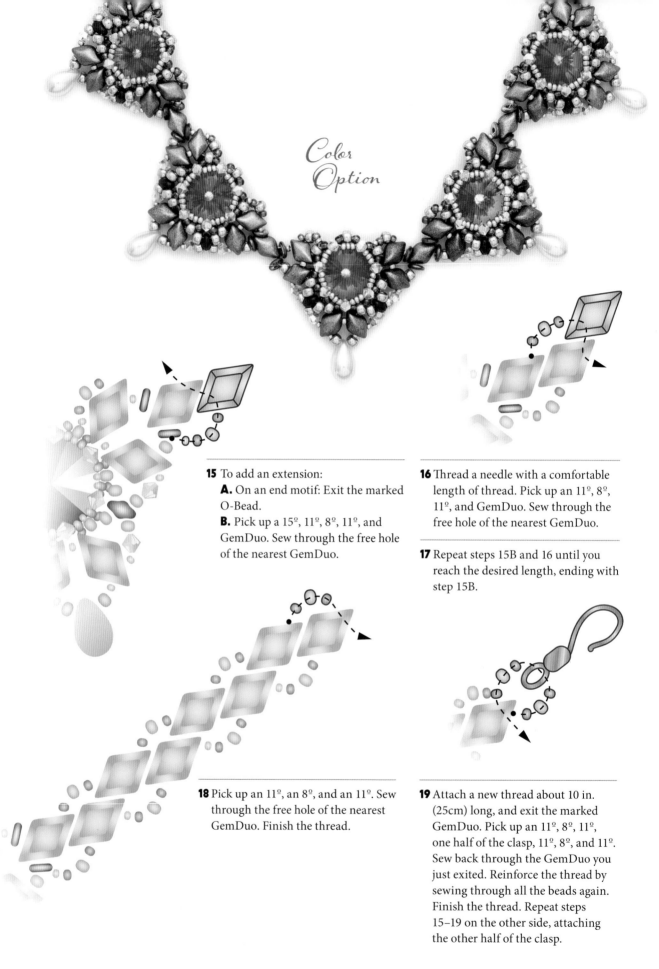

15 To add an extension:
   A. On an end motif: Exit the marked O-Bead.
   B. Pick up a 15º, 11º, 8º, 11º, and GemDuo. Sew through the free hole of the nearest GemDuo.

16 Thread a needle with a comfortable length of thread. Pick up an 11º, 8º, 11º, and GemDuo. Sew through the free hole of the nearest GemDuo.

17 Repeat steps 15B and 16 until you reach the desired length, ending with step 15B.

18 Pick up an 11º, an 8º, and an 11º. Sew through the free hole of the nearest GemDuo. Finish the thread.

19 Attach a new thread about 10 in. (25cm) long, and exit the marked GemDuo. Pick up an 11º, 8º, 11º, one half of the clasp, 11º, 8º, and 11º. Sew back through the GemDuo you just exited. Reinforce the thread by sewing through all the beads again. Finish the thread. Repeat steps 15–19 on the other side, attaching the other half of the clasp.

Vicki
Earrings

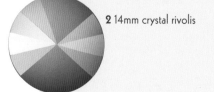
"A strong piece of jewelry can make a simple outfit look elegant."

— Giorgio Armani

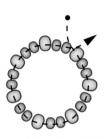

1 Thread a needle on a comfortable length of thread and pick up an 8º seed bead and two 11º seed beads seven times. Close the beads to a circle and knot twice.

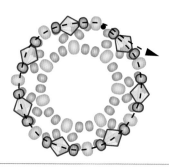

3 Pick up an 11º, 3mm bicone crystal, and 11º. Sew through the next 8º. Repeat around the ring. Finish by exiting the first 3mm crystal added.

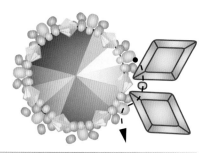

5 Pick up a GemDuo bead, 15º, and GemDuo. Sew through the next 8º. (Make sure the GemDuos are facing up!)

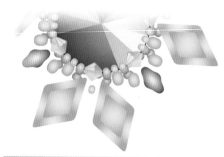

7 Repeat steps 5, 6, and 5.

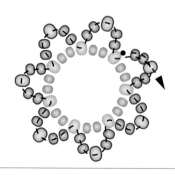

2 A. Sew through the nearest 8º.
B. Pick up two 11ºs, an 8º, and two 11ºs. Sew through the next 8º. Repeat around the ring.
C. At the end, step up through two 11ºs and the following 8º.

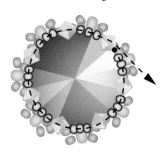

4 Place a 14mm rivoli in the beadwork, face-up. Pick up three 15ºs. Sew through the next 3mm crystal. Repeat around. At the end, step up through the adjacent 11º and the following 8º added in step 2B.

6 Pick up an 8º, MiniDuo bead, and 8º. Sew through the next 8º.

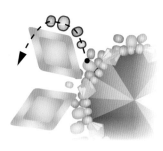

8 Pick up a 15º, 11º, 8º, and 11º. Sew through the free hole of the GemDuo to change direction.

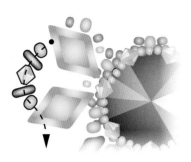

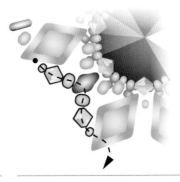

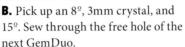

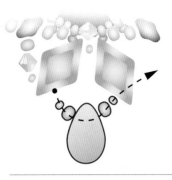

9 Pick up an 8º, O-Bead, 3mm crystal, O-Bead, and 8º. Sew through the free hole of the next GemDuo.

10 A. Pick up a 15º, 3mm crystal, and 8º. Sew through the free hole of the next MiniDuo.
B. Pick up an 8º, 3mm crystal, and 15º. Sew through the free hole of the next GemDuo.

11 Pick up a 15º, 8º, 6x9mm drop, 8º, and 15º. Sew through the free hole of the next GemDuo.

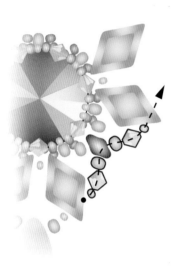

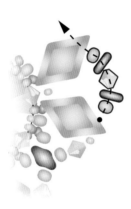

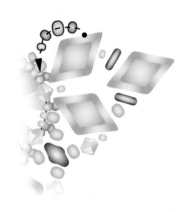

12 A. Pick up a 15º, 3mm crystal, and 8º. Sew through the free hole of the MiniDuo.
B. Pick up an 8º, 3mm crystal, and 15º. Sew through the free hole of the next GemDuo.

13 Pick up an 8º, O-Bead, 3mm crystal, O-Bead, and 8º. Sew through the free hole of the next GemDuo.

14 Pick up an 11º, 8º, 11º, and 15º. Sew through the marked 8º.

15 A. Sew to the back of the beadwork, and exit the top 8º.
B. Pick up five 15ºs, an earring finding, and five 15ºs. Close the beads to a circle by sewing through the same 8º. Reinforce the thread path, and end the thread.

16 Repeat to make a second earring.

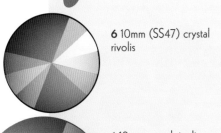

1g 15º seed beads

5g 11º seed beads

9g 8º seed beads

70 ZoliDuo beads, right version

70 ZoliDuo beads, left version

6 10mm (SS47) crystal rivolis

1 18mm crystal rivoli

Magnetic clasp

Beading thread and needle

"Never regret anything that makes you smile."

— Audrey Hepburn

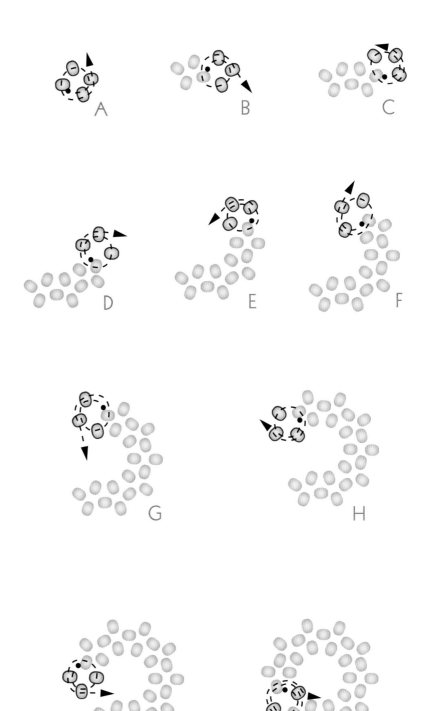

1 Thread a needle on a comfortable length of thread, and create a strip of right-angle weave using 8º seed beads as shown (see Techniques, p. 10). To close the beadwork into a circle, pick up an 8º, sew through the 8º at the starting end, pick up an 8º and sew through the 8º at this end. Retrace the thread path through the join. Exit the marked (interior) 8º.

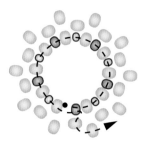

2 Pick up an 11º seed bead. Sew through the next 8º. Pick up a 15º seed bead. Sew through the next 8º. Repeat around the ring, alternating 11ºs and 15ºs. Sew through the beadwork to the other side. Finish by exiting an 8º on the outside.

3 Place a 10mm rivoli in the beadwork, face up. Pick up a 15º. Sew through the next 8º. Repeat around the ring. Retrace the thread path to reinforce the work. Finish by exiting an 8º. End the thread.

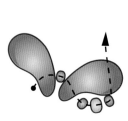

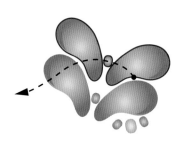

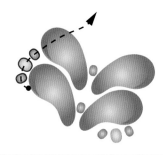

4 Start a new thread. Pick up a ZoliDuo (left, concave side), 11º, ZoliDuo bead (right, convex side), 11º, 8º, and 11º (make sure the ZoliDuos are facing up). Sew through the free hole of the ZoliDuo just added.

5 Pick up a ZoliDuo (right, concave side), 11º, and ZoliDuo (left, convex side). Sew through the free hole of the next ZoliDuo.

6 Pick up an 11º, 8º, and 11º. Sew through the free hole of the last ZoliDuo added in the previous step.

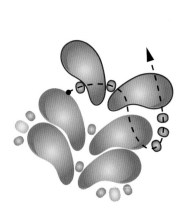

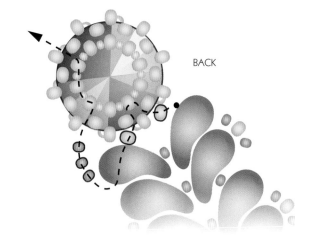

BACK

7 A. Pick up an 11º, ZoliDuo (left, concave side), 11º, and ZoliDuo (right, convex side). Sew through the free hole of the next ZoliDuo.
B. Pick up three 11ºs. Sew through the free hole of the ZoliDuo above.
C. Repeat step 5–7B until you have eight pairs of ZoliDuos, ending and adding thread as needed. Finish at step 6.

8 Turn your work to the back side. Attach the rivoli (back view):
A. Pick up an 8º. Sew directly through an 8º on the back of the rivoli as shown.
B. Pick up an 8º. Sew through the free hole of the adjacent end ZoliDuo.
C. Pick up three 11ºs. Sew through the marked beads on the back of the rivoli. Finish by exiting the marked 8º.

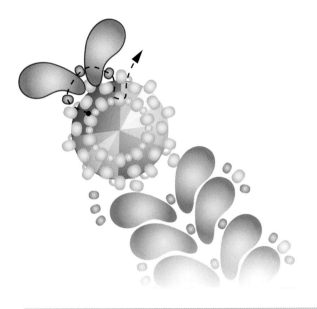

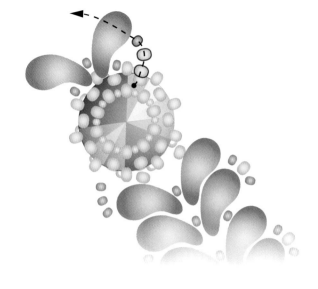

9 Back view: Pick up an 11º, ZoliDuo (right, concave side), 11º, ZoliDuo (left, convex side), and 11º (make sure the ZoliDuos are facing the correct way). Sew through the marked 8º.

10 Pick up two 8ºs, and an 11º. Sew through the free hole of the adjacent ZoliDuo. Turn your work face up.

11 Repeat from steps 5–7B until you have nine pairs of ZoliDuos. Finish at step 6. Bezel and attach another rivoli as in steps 8–10.

12 Repeat until you reach half the length of the necklace (three rivolis). Finish this half at step 6.

13 A. Make the other strip as the mirror image of the first strip: Start a new thread. Pick up a ZoliDuo (right), 11º, ZoliDuo (left), 11º, 8º, and 11º. Sew through the free hole of the ZoliDuo you just added.
B. Pick up a ZoliDuo (left), an 11º, and a ZoliDuo (right). Sew through the free hole of the next ZoliDuo.
C. Pick up an 11º, 8º, and 11º. Sew through the free hole of the last ZoliDuo you added in the previous step.
D. Pick up an 11º, ZoliDuo (right), 11º, and ZoliDuo (left). Sew through the free hole of the next ZoliDuo (left).
E. Pick up three 11ºs, and sew through the free hole of the ZoliDuo above.
F. Repeat B–E until you have eight pairs of ZoliDuos. Finish at C.
G. Attach a rivoli as in step 8: Working on the back, pick up an 8º. Sew directly through an 8º on the back of the rivoli. Pick up an 8º. Sew through the free hole of the adjacent end ZoliDuo. Pick up three 11ºs. Sew through the marked beads on the back of the rivoli. Finish by exiting the marked 8º.
H. Continue as in step 9: Working on the back, pick up an 11º, ZoliDuo (left), 11º, ZoliDuo (right), and 11º. Sew through the marked 8º.
I. Work as in step 10: Pick up two 8ºs and an 11º. Sew through the free hole of the adjacent ZoliDuo.
J. Repeat B–E until you have nine pairs of ZoliDuos. Finish at C. Attach another rivoli as shown in G–I. Repeat until you reach half the length of the necklace (three rivolis). Finish this half at C.

 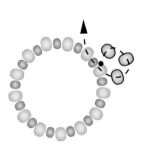 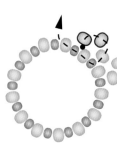

14 Pick up an 8º and an 11º, 13 times. Sew through all the beads again, knot twice, and exit the next 8º.

15 Pick up three 8ºs. Sew back through the 8º you just exited. Continue through the next 11º and the following 8º.

16 Pick up two 8ºs. Sew through the marked beads. Repeat this step around the ring as shown. Finish by exiting the marked 8º.

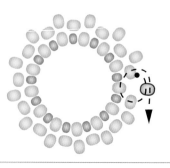 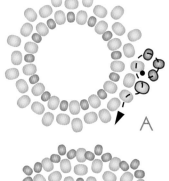 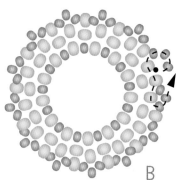 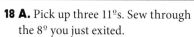 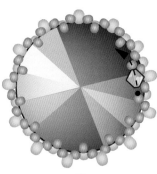 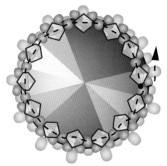

17 Pick up an 8º. Sew through the marked beads. Finish by exiting the 8º you just added.

18 A. Pick up three 11ºs. Sew through the 8º you just exited.
B. Pick up an 8º. Sew through the next 8º.
C. Repeat step 18A–B around the ring. Exit the marked 11º.

19 Insert a 18mm rivoli into beadwork face up. Pick up a 3mm bicone crystal. Sew through the center 11º in the next set of three 11ºs. Repeat this step around the ring, and step up through an outer 8º.

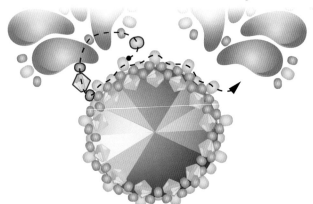 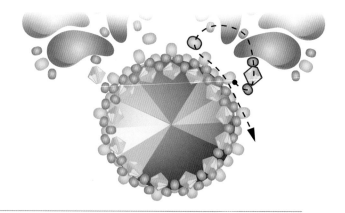

20 Pick up an 8º. Sew through the 11º, ZoliDuo, 11º, and ZoliDuo on the left half of the necklace. Pick up an 11º, 3mm bicone crystal, and 11º. Sew through nine 8ºs on the rivoli.

21 Pick up an 11º, 3mm bicone crystal, and 11º. Sew through the ZoliDuo, 11º, ZoliDuo, and 11º on the right half of the necklace. Pick up an 8º. Sew through the last three 8ºs from step 18. Finish the thread.

22 Attach a new thread about 10 in. (25cm) long. Exit the
marked ZoliDuo. Pick up an 11°, 8°, 11°, one half of the
clasp, 11°, 8° and 11°. Sew through the free hole of the
other ZoliDuo. Pick up an 11°. Sew back through the same
hole of this ZoliDuo. Reinforce the clasp attachment by
going through all the beads just added once more. Finish
the thread. Repeat on the other side to attach the other
half of the clasp.

Color
Option

Darwin's Orchid
Pendant

SUPPLIES

- ⬤ **.5g** 15º seed beads
- ⬤ **2g** 11º seed beads
- ⬤ **1g** 8º seed beads
- ⬤ **7** SuperDuo beads
- ◇ **14** GemDuo beads
- ⬤ **18** 4mm fire-polished beads
- ◇ **7** 4mm bicone crystals
- ⬤ **12** 3mm pearls

1 22x30mm fancy oval stone

1 11x10mm crystal briolette

Beading needle and thread

"Each design is a piece of my heart and a small piece of my life."
— Isabella

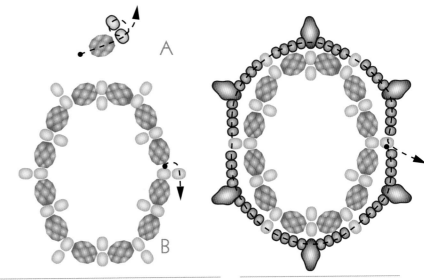

1 A. Thread a needle on a comfortable length of thread. Pick up a 4mm fire-polished bead and two 8º seed beads. Sew through the first 8º picked up.
B. Repeat step 1A, 11 times. Sew through the first fire-polished bead picked up. Retrace the thread path through all the beads again. Tie a surgeon's knot. Finish by exiting the second 8º you added in the first step, changing work direction.

2 Pick up four 11º seed beads, a SuperDuo bead, and four 11ºs. Skip the next set of 8º, and sew through an 8º in following pair of 8ºs. Repeat around five times exiting the first 8º.

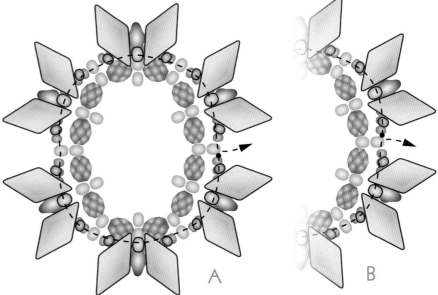

3 A. Pick up an 11º, GemDuo bead, 8º, GemDuo, and 11º. (Make sure the GemDuos are facing up.) Skip the next SuperDuo, and sew through the following 8º.
B. Repeat around. Finish by exiting the first 8º again.
C. Insert a 22x30mm fancy oval stone in the beadwork, face up.

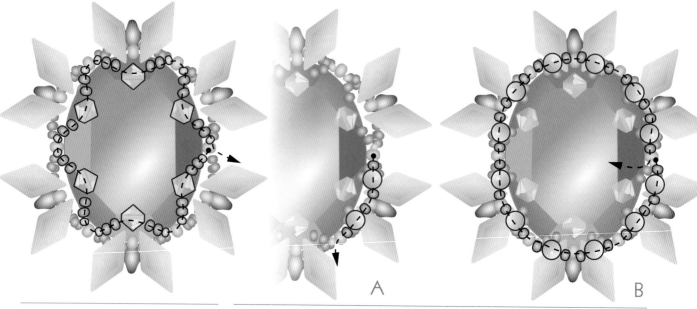

A

B

4 Pick up a 15º seed bead, two 11ºs, 4mm bicone crystal, two 11ºs, and 15º. Skip the next 8º pair, and sew through the nearest 8º in the next pair. Repeat around. Finish by exiting the first 8º again.

5 A. Pick up an 11º, 3mm pearl, and 11º. Sew through the next 8º (between the GemDuos).
   B. Pick up an 11º, 3mm pearl, and 11º. Sew through the next 8º.
   C. Repeat steps 5A–B around. Finish by exiting the first 11º added in this round.

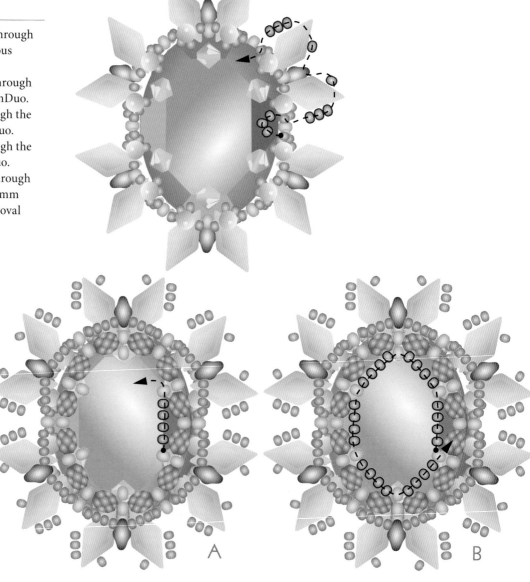

6 A. Pick up three 11ºs. Sew through the 11º in front of the previous 3mm pearl.
   B. Pick up three 11ºs. Sew through the free hole of the next GemDuo.
   C. Pick up an 11º. Sew through the free hole of the next SuperDuo.
   D. Pick up an 11º. Sew through the free hole of the next GemDuo.
   E. Pick up three 11ºs. Sew through the 11º in front of the next 3mm pearl, exiting the face of the oval fancy stone.
   F. Repeat around step 5A–E.

7 A. Sew to the back side of the beadwork. Exit a free 8º, as shown.
   B. Pick up four 11ºs. Sew through the next free 8º.
   C. Repeat around and finish the thread.

A

B

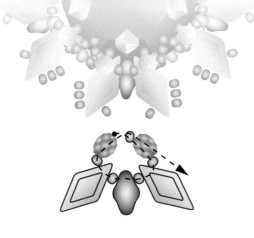

8 Cut a new thread about 20 in. (51cm) long. Pick up an 11º, fire-polished bead, 11º, GemDuo, 11º, SuperDuo, 11º, GemDuo, 11º, and fire-polished bead. (Make sure the GemDuos are facing up!) Close the beads to a circle. Tie a surgeon's knot. Finish by exiting the first fire-polished bead.

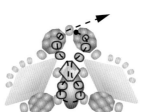

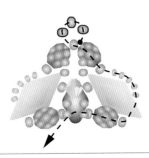

9 A. Pick up five 15º seed beads. Sew through the free hole of the next GemDuo.
B. Pick up an 11º, fire-polished bead, and 11º. Sew through the free hole of the SuperDuo.
C. Pick up an 11º, fire-polished bead, and 11º. Sew through the free hole of the next GemDuo.
D. Pick up five 15ºs. Sew through the fire-polished bead and the following 11º.

10 A. Pick up a 15ºs, two 11ºs, 4mm bicone crystal, and two 11ºs. Sew through the same hole of the SuperDuo as in step 9B.
B. Pick up two 11ºs. Sew back through the crystal.
C. Pick up two 11ºs and a 15º, and sew through the first 11º again.

11 Pick up three 11ºs. Sew through the 11º your thread just exited to make a picot, and continue through the marked beads. Finish by exiting the SuperDuo.

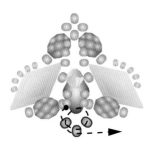

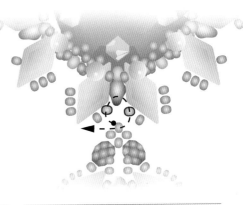

12 Pick up three 11ºs. Sew through the SuperDuo again to make a picot. Continue through the next two 11ºs.

13 Pick up an 11º, fire-polished bead, 11º, 11x10mm briolette, 11º, fire-polished bead, and 11º. Sew through the 11º your thread exited at the start of this step. Continue up through the marked beads to exit the top 11º.

14 A. Connect the drop motif to the work: Pick an 11º. Sew through the bottom SuperDuo as shown.
B. Pick an 11º. Sew through the first 11º again. Reinforce the work, and end the thread.

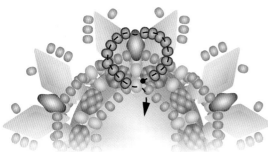

15 To add a hanging loop, sew through the beadwork to exit the marked 8º on the back of the pendant.
A. Pick up eight 8ºs, and sew through the adjacent SuperDuo.
B. Pick up eight 8ºs, and sew through the 8º your thread exited at the start of this step. Retrace the thread path through the loop, and finish the thread.

Tulip
Necklace

SUPPLIES

- **3g** 15º seed beads
- **10g** 11º seed beads
- **34** 4mm bicone crystals
- **34** SuperDuo beads
- **70** GemDuo beads
- **142** 4mm fire-polished beads
- **1** 11x18mm drop bead, vertical hole
- Magnetic clasp
- Beading needle and thread

"Jewelry has the power to make you feel special and your moments unique."

— Isabella

1 Thread a needle on a comfortable length of thread, and pick up four 11º seed beads. Leaving a 10 in. (25cm) tail, tie the beads into a ring using a surgeon's knot, and sew through the first two 11ºs.

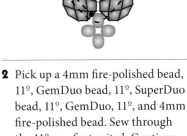

2 Pick up a 4mm fire-polished bead, 11º, GemDuo bead, 11º, SuperDuo bead, 11º, GemDuo, 11º, and 4mm fire-polished bead. Sew through the 11º you first exited. Continue through the following fire-polished bead. (Make sure the GemDuos are facing up!)

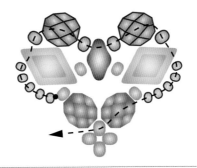

3 A. Pick up five 15ºs. Sew through the GemDuo.
B. Pick up an 11º, fire-polished bead, and 11º. Sew through the available hole of the SuperDuo.
C. Pick up an 11º, fire-polished bead, and 11º. Sew through the next GemDuo.
D. Pick up five 15ºs. Sew through the fire-polished bead and the following 11º.

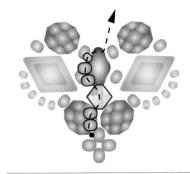

4 Pick up two 11ºs, 4mm bicone crystal, two 11ºs, and 15º. Sew through the same hole of the SuperDuo as in step 3B.

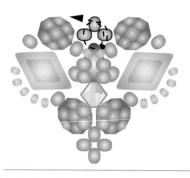

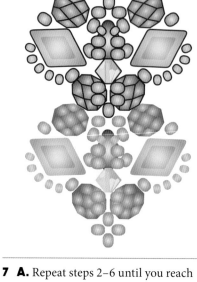

5 Pick up a 15º and two 11ºs. Sew back through the 4mm bicone crystal. Pick up two 11ºs. Sew through the 11º where you began in step 4. Continue through the marked beads, and finish by exiting the SuperDuo.

6 Pick up three 11ºs. Sew through the SuperDuo you just exited. Continue through the next two 11ºs.

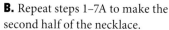

7 A. Repeat steps 2–6 until you reach half the length of the necklace, ending and adding threading as needed. Finish at step 6.
B. Repeat steps 1–7A to make the second half of the necklace.

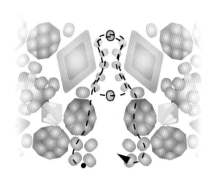

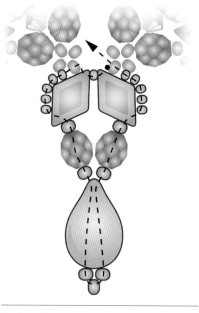

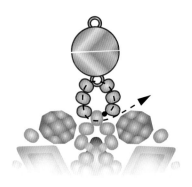

8 A. Attaching the starting point of both half strips: With the tail of one strip, sew through the marked beads to exit five 15ºs in the same strip.
B. Pick up a 15º. Sew through the five 15ºs of the second strip. Pick up another 15º. Sew through the five 15ºs of the first strip where you started. Sew through the first 15º you added in this step, and continue through five 15ºs in the second strip, and down through the marked beads to exit an 11º, as shown.

9 A. Pick up a GemDuo, a 15º, and a GemDuo. Sew through the corresponding 11º on the first strip.
B. Pick up five 15ºs. Sew through the free hole of the nearest GemDuo.
C. Pick up an 11º, fire-polished bead, 11º, 11x18mm vertical-hole drop bead, and three 11ºs. Sew back through the drop.
D. Pick up an 11º, fire-polished bead, and 11º. Sew through the free hole of the first GemDuo added in step 9A.
E. Pick up five 15ºs. Sew through the 11º your thread exited at the start of step 9A. Finish the threads.

10 Attach a new thread about 10 in. (25cm) long. Exit the center 11º at one end of the necklace. Pick up three 11ºs, half of the clasp, and three 11ºs. Sew back through the first 11º. Sew through all the beads again to reinforce. Finish the thread. Repeat on the other side of the necklace to attach the other half of the clasp.

Sunset Gem
Pendant

.5g 15º seed beads

1g 11º seed bead

6 GemDuo beads

12 SuperDuo beads

6 4mm fire-polished beads

6 4mm bicone crystals

1 27mm round crystal stone (Swarovski Article 1201)

Beading thread and needle

"Don't give up. The beginning is always the hardest. Life rewards those who work hard to accomplish their dream."
— Unknown

1 Thread a needle on a comfortable length of thread, and pick up a 4mm fire-polished bead and an 11º seed bead, 12 times. Sew through the beads again. Tie a surgeon's knot. Continue through the next fire-polished bead and the following 11º.

2 Pick up three 11ºs. Sew through the 11º again. Continue through the next 4mm fire-polished bead and 11º. Repeat around the ring. At the end, step up though the first two 11ºs added in this step.

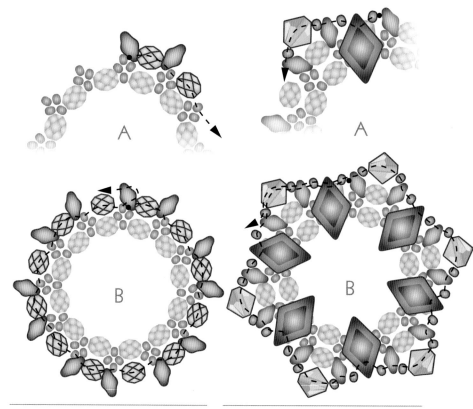

3 A. Pick up a SuperDuo, 4mm fire-polished bead, and SuperDuo. Sew through the next 11º. Pick up a 4mm fire-polished bead. Sew through the next 11º.

B. Repeat step 3A around the ring. Finish by exiting the first SuperDuo you added. Sew back through the free hole (changing work directions).

4 A. Pick up an 11º, GemDuo bead, and 11º. Sew through the free hole of the next SuperDuo. Pick up an 11º, 4mm bicone crystal, and 11º. Sew through the free hole of the following SuperDuo.

B. Repeat step 4A around the ring. Finish by exiting the first 11º, the 4mm bicone, and the 11º.

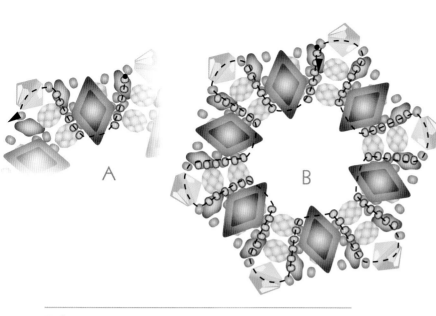

A

B

5 **A.** Insert a 27mm round crystal stone into the beadwork. Pick up six 15º seed beads, and sew through the free hole of the next GemDuo. This hole will be toward the inside edge of the ring. Pick up six 15ºs. Sew through the free hole of the next 11º, 4mm bicone crystal, and 11º.
B. Repeat step 5A around. Finish by exiting the first two 15ºs you added in this step.

Color Option

6 Pick up two 11ºs, skip the adjacent bicone and the following two 15ºs, and sew through the next four 15ºs, GemDuo, and four 15ºs. Repeat around the ring.

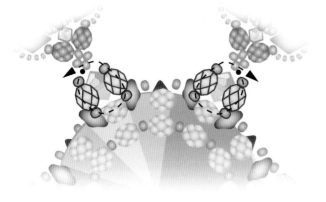

7 To add a single hanging loop, exit a SuperDuo as shown. Pick up six 11ºs. Sew through the next SuperDuo. Finish the thread. If you plan to attach the pendant to a beaded necklace, as shown above, skip this step and move on to step 8.

8 To connect this pendant to the Tulip Necklace, p. 76, thread a needle on the tail of one strip on the Tulip Necklace. Exit the bottom 11º.
A. Pick up an 11º, 4mm fire-polished bead, and 11º. Sew through a fire-polished bead on the back of the pendant.
B. Pick up an 11º, fire-polished bead, and 11º. Sew through the 11º on the necklace. Reinforce the connection. Finish the thread. Repeat this step to connect the second half of the necklace, referring to the illustration for placement.

Empera
Necklace

4g 15º seed beads

 10g 11º seed beads

 **11g** 8º seed beads

 190 3mm bicone crystals

90 GemDuo beads

22 5x10mm crystal navettes

11 14mm crystal rivolis

1 11x10mm crystal briolette

Hook clasp

Beading needle and thread

"I didn't get there by wishing for it or hoping for it, but by working for it."

— Estée Lauder

1 Thread a needle on a comfortable length of thread, and pick up an 8º seed bead and two 11º seed beads seven times. Sew through the beads again, and tie a surgeon's knot. Exit an 8º.

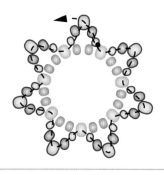

2 Pick up a 15º seed bead, 11º, 8º, 11º, and 15º. Sew through the next 8º. Repeat around the ring. At the end, step up through the first 15º, 11º, and 8º added in this step.

3 Insert a 14mm rivoli into the bead-work, face up. Pick up a 15º, 3mm bicone crystal, and 15º. Sew through the next 8º. Repeat around the ring. Finish by exiting the first 3mm bicone crystal you added.

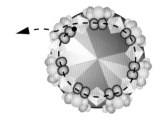

4 Pick up two 11ºs. Sew through the next 3mm bicone crystal. Repeat around the ring. Sew through all the beads again to reinforce. At the end, step down and exit the 8º next to the rivoli.

5 A. Pick up an 11º, 8º, 5x10mm navette, and 8º. (Make sure the navette is facing up!) Sew through the next 8º.
B. Pick up an 8º, navette, 8º, and 11º. Sew through the next 8º.

6 Pick up an 11º, 8º, 3mm bicone crystal, and 11º. Sew through the free hole of the navette.

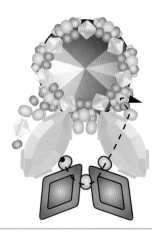

7 Pick up an 8º, GemDuo bead, 8º, GemDuo, and 8º. Sew diagonally through the next navette. Continue through the following 8º, 11º, and 8º next to the rivoli.

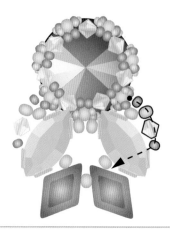

8 Pick up an 11º, 8º, 3mm bicone crystal, and 11º. Sew through the free hole of the navette.

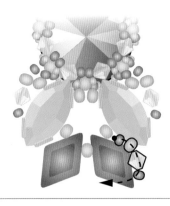

9 Pick up an 11º, 8º, 3mm bicone crystal, and 11º. Sew through the free hole of the GemDuo.

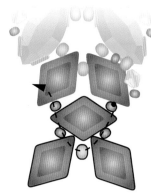
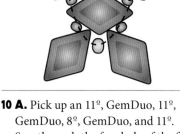
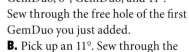

10 A. Pick up an 11º, GemDuo, 11º, GemDuo, 8º, GemDuo, and 11º. Sew through the free hole of the first GemDuo you just added.
B. Pick up an 11º. Sew through the free hole of the next GemDuo.

11 Pick up an 11º, 3mm bicone crystal, 8º, and 11º. Sew through the navette and the following marked beads, exiting the 8º next to the rivoli.

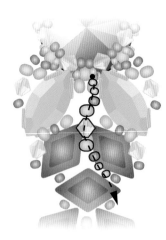

12 Pick up two 15ºs, an 11º, 8º, 3mm bicone crystal, 8º, 11º, and two 15ºs. Sew through the center GemDuo.

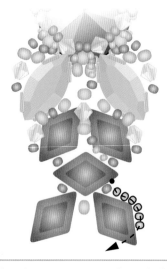

13 Pick up six 15ºs. Sew through the free hole of the right GemDuo.

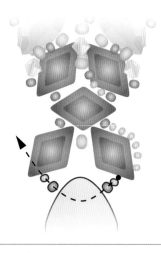

14 Pick up a 15º, 11º, 11x10mm briolette, 11º, and 15º. Sew through the free hole of the left GemDuo.

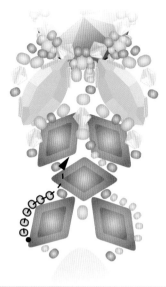

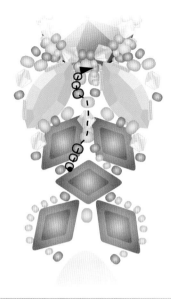

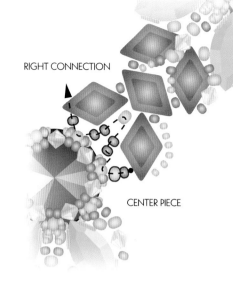

RIGHT CONNECTION

CENTER PIECE

15 Pick up six 15ºs. Sew through the marked GemDuo.

16 A. Pick up two 15ºs and an 11º. Sew back through the 8º, 3mm bicone crystal, and 8º.
B. Pick up an 11º and two 15ºs. Sew through the 8º you exited in step 12. Finish the thread.

17 Connect the motif on the right of the center piece:
A. Create a new motif by following steps 1–13.
B. Pick up an 11º and an 8º. Sew through the marked 8º on the rivoli.
C. Pick up two 11ºs. Sew through the 8º between GemDuos.
D. Pick up two 11ºs. Sew through the marked 8º on the rivoli.
E. Pick up an 11º. Sew through the nearest GemDuo.

CENTER PIECE

18 Repeat steps 15–16. Finish the thread.

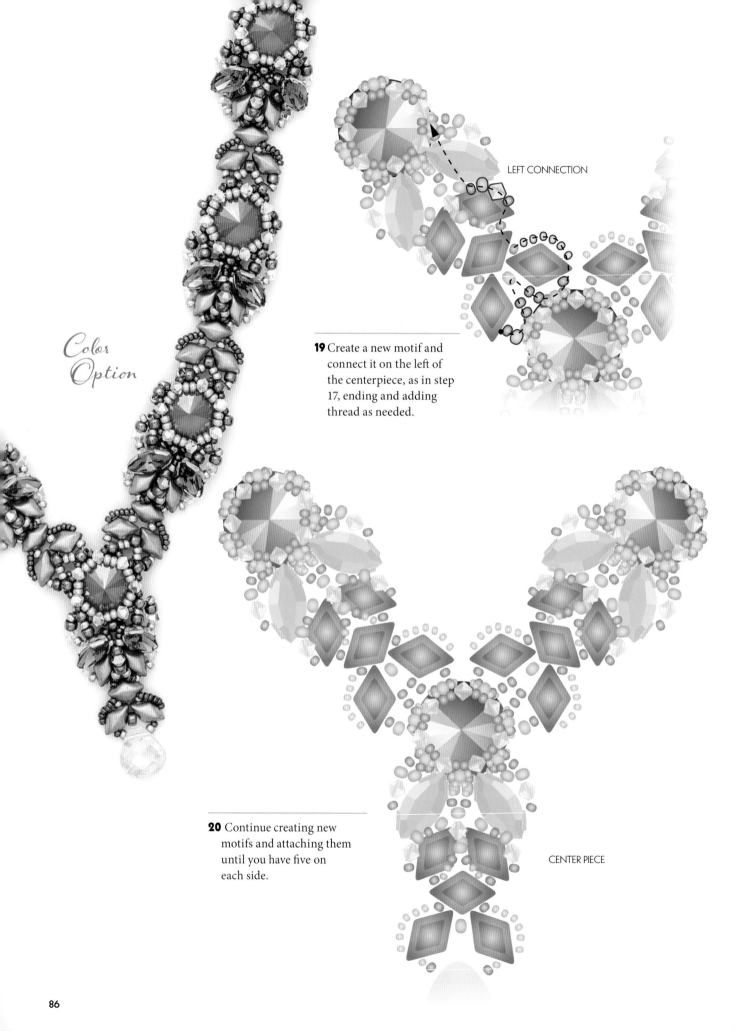

LEFT CONNECTION

19 Create a new motif and connect it on the left of the centerpiece, as in step 17, ending and adding thread as needed.

20 Continue creating new motifs and attaching them until you have five on each side.

CENTER PIECE

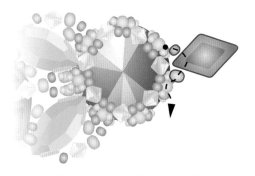

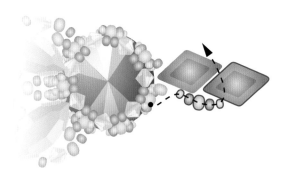

21 Attach a new thread about 20 in. (51cm) long to the rivoli, exiting the marked 8º. Pick up an 11º, GemDuo, and 8º. Sew through the next 8º next to the rivoli. (Make sure the GemDuo is facing up!)

22 Pick up a 15º, 11º, 8º, 11º, 15º, and GemDuo. Sew through the free hole of the previous GemDuo.

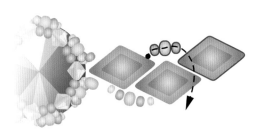

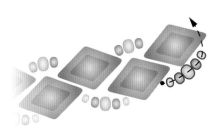

23 Pick up an 11º, 8º, 11º, and GemDuo. Sew through the free hole of the previous GemDuo.

24 Repeat steps 22–23 until you reach the desired length. Finish at step 23. Pick up a 15º, 11º, 8º, 11º, and 15º. Sew through the free hole of the GemDuo. Finish the thread.

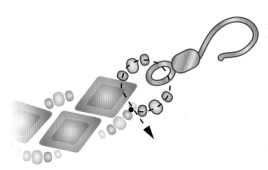

25 Attach a new thread about 10 in. (25cm) long. Sew through the beads, and exit a GemDuo and the following 15º. Pick up an 11º, 8º, 11º, one half of the clasp, 11º, 8º, and 11º. Sew through the GemDuo and 15º you first exited. Reinforce the work by sewing through all the beads again. Finish the thread.

26 Repeat steps 21–25 on the other side of the necklace.

Empera
Earrings

SUPPLIES

 .5g 15º seed beads

 2g 11º seed beads

 2g 8º seed beads

 24 3mm bicone crystals

 10 GemDuo beads

 4 5x10mm crystal navettes

 2 14mm crystal rivolis

2 11x10mm crystal briolettes

1 pair of earring hooks

Beading needle and thread

"Wearing jewelry should make you feel classy and fabulous."

— Isabella

1 Thread a needle on a comfortable length of thread, and pick up an 8º seed bead and two 11º seed beads seven times. Sew through the beads again, and tie a surgeon's knot. Exit an 8º.

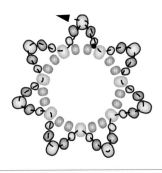

2 Pick up a 15º seed bead, 11º, 8º, 11º, and 15º. Sew through the next 8º. Repeat around the ring. Step up through the first 15º, 11º, and 8º.

3 Insert a 14mm rivoli into the bead-work face up. Pick up a 15º, 3mm bicone crystal, and 15º. Sew through the next 8º. Repeat around the ring. Finish by exiting the first 3mm bicone crystal you added.

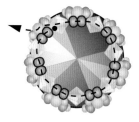

4 Pick up two 11ºs. Sew through the next 3mm bicone crystal. Repeat around the ring. Sew through all the beads again to reinforce. At the end, step down to exit an 8º.

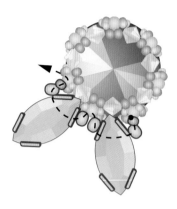

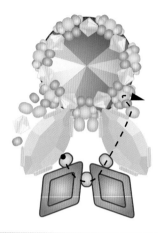

5 A. Pick up an 11º, 8º, 5x10mm navette, and 8º. Sew through the next existing 8º. (Make sure the navettes are facing up!)
B. Pick up an 8º, navette, 8º, and 11º. Sew through the next existing 8º.

6 Pick up an 11º, 8º, 3mm bicone crystal, and 11º. Sew through the free hole of the navette.

7 Pick up an 8º, GemDuo bead, 8º, GemDuo, and 8º. Sew diagonally through the next navette.

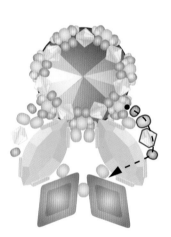

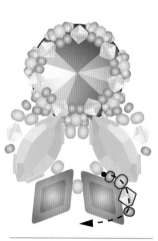

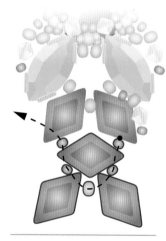

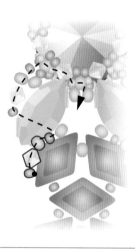

8 Pick up an 11º, 8º, 3mm bicone crystal, and 11º. Sew through the free hole of the navette.

9 Pick up an 11º, 8º, 3mm bicone crystal, and 11º. Sew through the free hole of the GemDuo.

10 A. Pick up an 11º, GemDuo, 11º, GemDuo, 8º, GemDuo, and 11º. Sew through the free hole of the first GemDuo you just added. (Make sure the GemDuos are facing up!)
B. Pick up an 11º. Sew through the free hole of the next existing GemDuo.

11 Pick up an 11º, 3mm bicone crystal, 8º, and 11º. Sew through the navette and the following marked beads, exiting the 8º next to the rivoli.

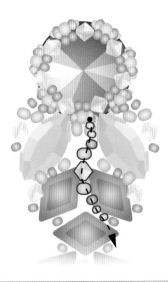

12 Pick up two 15ºs, an 11º, 8º, 3mm bicone crystal, 8º, 11º, and two 15ºs. Sew through the center GemDuo.

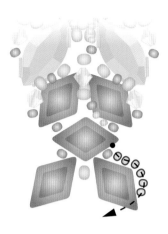

13 Pick up six 15ºs. Sew through the free hole of the right GemDuo.

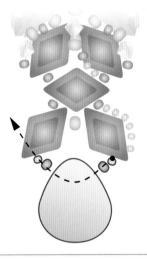

14 Pick up a 15º, 11º, briolette, 11º, and 15º. Sew through the free hole of the left GemDuo.

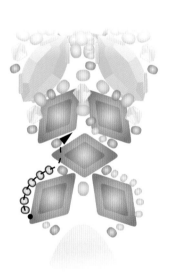

15 Pick up six 15ºs and an 11º. Sew through the marked GemDuo.

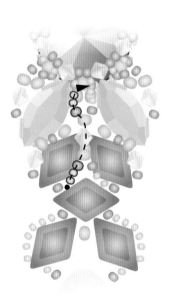

16 A. Pick up two 15ºs and an 11º. Sew back through the 8º, 3mm bicone crystal, and 8º.
B. Pick up an 11º and two 15ºs. Sew through the 8º you exited in step 12. Finish the thread.

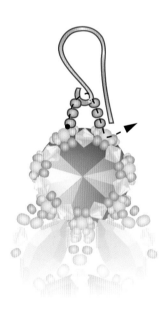

17 Sew through the beadwork to exit the marked 8º. Pick up three 11ºs, an earring hook, and three 11ºs. Sew through the next 8º. Finish the thread. Repeat to make a second earring.

Tereza
Necklace

SUPPLIES

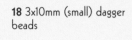 **4g** 15º seed beads

11g 11º seed beads

 **16g** 8º seed beads

220 3mm pearls

25 3mm bicone crystals

40 4mm bicone crystals

18 3x10mm (small) dagger beads

9 5x16mm (large) dagger beads

 **16** 10mm (SS47) crystal rivolis

6 14mm crystal rivolis

3 18mm crystal rivolis

1 magnetic clasp

Beading needle and thread

"Wearing a Swarovski design is a great way to leave a little unforgettable sparkle wherever you go."
— Isabella

1 Make the 18mm rivoli bezel: Thread a needle on a comfortable length of thread, and pick up an 8º seed bead and two 11º seed beads, 10 times. Sew through all the beads again, and tie a surgeon's knot. Exit two 11ºs.

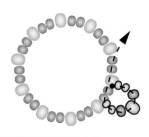

2 Pick up two 15º seed beads, 11º, 8º, 11º, and two 15ºs. Sew through the same two 11ºs. Continue through the following 8º and next two 11ºs.

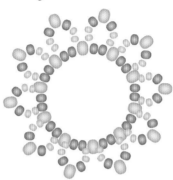

3 Repeat around the ring. At the end, step up through two 15ºs, 11º, and 8º.

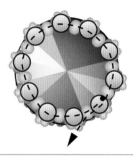

4 Insert an 18mm rivoli into the beadwork, face up. Pick up a 3mm pearl, and sew through the next 8º. Repeat around the ring. Sew through all the beads again to reinforce.

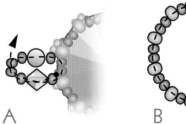

A   B

5 Sew to the back side of the rivoli. Exit two 11ºs.
   A. Pick up an 11º, 3mm bicone crystal, four 11ºs, 3mm pearl, and 11º. Sew through the two 11ºs you first exited. Continue through the beads, exiting the two marked 11ºs.
   B. Pick up an 8º and two 11ºs nine times, then pick up another 8º. Sew through the two 11ºs you just exited to form a ring.

6 Repeat steps 2–4.

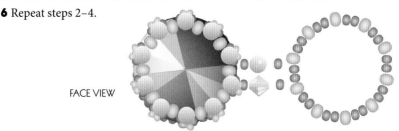

FACE VIEW

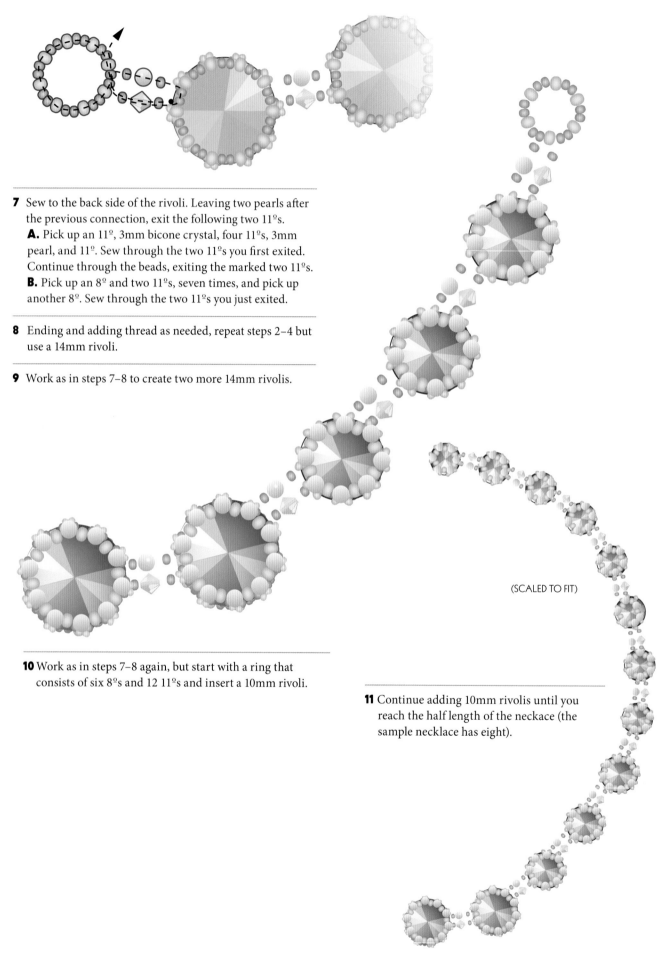

7 Sew to the back side of the rivoli. Leaving two pearls after the previous connection, exit the following two 11°s.
   A. Pick up an 11°, 3mm bicone crystal, four 11°s, 3mm pearl, and 11°. Sew through the two 11°s you first exited. Continue through the beads, exiting the marked two 11°s.
   B. Pick up an 8° and two 11°s, seven times, and pick up another 8°. Sew through the two 11°s you just exited.

8 Ending and adding thread as needed, repeat steps 2–4 but use a 14mm rivoli.

9 Work as in steps 7–8 to create two more 14mm rivolis.

(SCALED TO FIT)

10 Work as in steps 7–8 again, but start with a ring that consists of six 8°s and 12 11°s and insert a 10mm rivoli.

11 Continue adding 10mm rivolis until you reach the half length of the neckace (the sample necklace has eight).

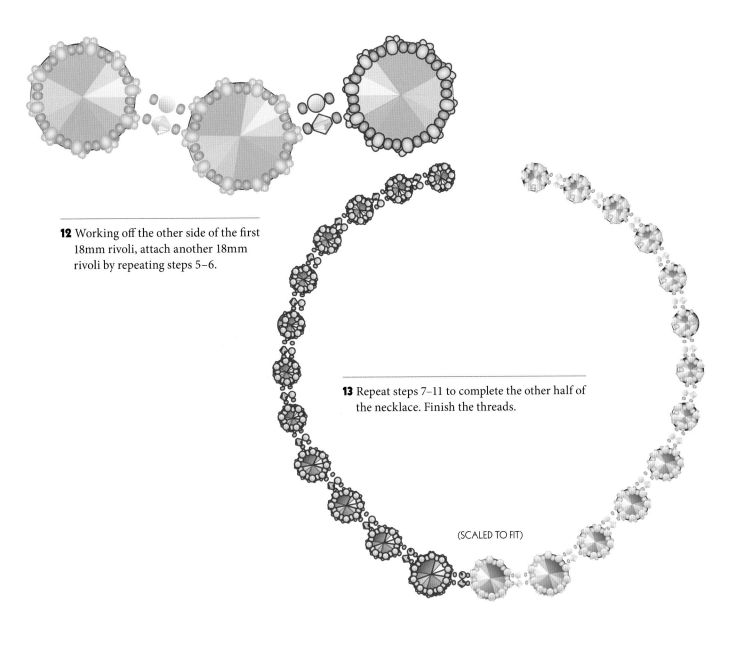

12 Working off the other side of the first 18mm rivoli, attach another 18mm rivoli by repeating steps 5–6.

13 Repeat steps 7–11 to complete the other half of the necklace. Finish the threads.

(SCALED TO FIT)

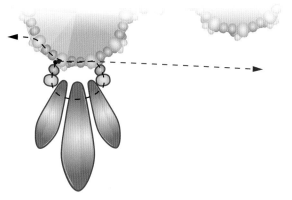

14 Work on the back side, and attach a new thread (about 1 yd./.9m) to the center 18mm rivoli. You will use half of the thread for the right side and the other half for the left side. Exit an 8º as shown. Pick up an 11º, 8º, small dagger, large dagger, small dagger, 8º, and 11º. Sew through the previous 8º and the following two 11ºs and an 8º. Continue through the next two 11ºs and the following 8º.

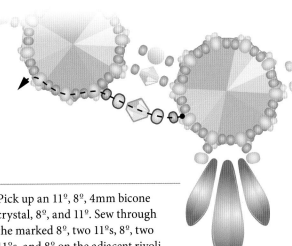

15 Pick up an 11º, 8º, 4mm bicone crystal, 8º, and 11º. Sew through the marked 8º, two 11ºs, 8º, two 11ºs, and 8º on the adjacent rivoli, as shown.

Color
Option

16 A. Pick up an 11º, 8º, small dagger, large dagger, small dagger, 8º, and 11º. Sew through the previous 8º, two 11ºs, and 8º.

B. Pick up an 11º, 8º, 4mm bicone crystal, 8º, and 11º. Sew through the marked 8º, two 11ºs, 8º, and 11º on the next 14mm rivoli, as shown.

C. Repeat steps 16A–16B on the remaining 14mm rivolis. Finish the working thread tail.

D. Repeat steps 15–16C on the other side.

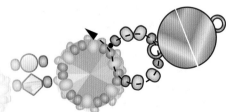

17 Attach a new thread about 10 in. (25cm). Sew through the beads and exit an 11º. Pick up an 11º, two 8ºs, 11º, one half of the clasp, 11º, two 8ºs, and 11º. Close the beads to a circle. Sew through the previous 11º, 8º, and 11º. Reinforce by sewing through all the beads again, and finish the thread. Repeat this step on the other side of the necklace to attach the other half of the clasp.

Tereza Earrings

SUPPLIES

- **.5g** 15º seed beads

- **2g** 11º seed beads

- **1g** 8º seed beads

- **16** 3mm pearls

- **2** 3x10mm (small) dagger beads

- **4** 5x16mm (large) dagger beads

- **2** 14mm crystal rivolis

Pair of earring hooks

Beading needle and thread

"You always
deserve new jewelry."
— Isabella

1 Make the 14mm rivoli bezel: Thread a needle on a comfortable length of thread, and pick up an 8º seed bead and two 11º seed beads, eight times. Sew through the beads again, and tie a surgeon's knot. Exit two 11ºs.

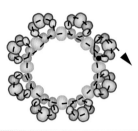

2 Pick up a 15º seed bead, 11º, 8º, 11º, and 15º. Sew through the same two 11ºs. Continue through the following 8º and next two 11ºs. Repeat around the ring. Step up through the first 15º, 11º, and 8º.

3 Insert a 14mm rivoli face up. Pick up a 3mm pearl. Sew through the next 8º. Repeat around the ring. Sew through all the beads again to reinforce. Finish by exiting an 8º.

4 Sew through the beads to the back, and exit the beadwork between two 11ºs. Pick up an 11º, 8º, small dagger bead, large dagger bead, small dagger, 8º, and 11º. Skip the next 11º, 8º, and 11º, and sew the following 11º beads to exit the top 8º and the following 11º, as shown.

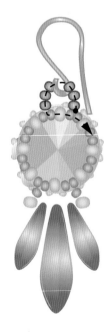

5 Pick up three 11ºs, an earring hook, and three 11ºs. Sew through the next 11º, 8º, and 11º. Continue through the beads on the back side. Reinforce the work by sewing through all the beads again. Finish the thread. Repeat to make a second earring.

SUPPLIES

- ⬤ .5g 15º seed beads
- ⬤ 8g 11º seed beads
- ⬤ 23g 8º seed beads
- ◯ 60 3mm pearls
- ◇ 19 4mm bicone crystals
- ◈ 19 6mm rose montées
- ⬭ 19 6x9mm or 5x7mm drop beads, top-drilled

Magnetic clasp

Beading needle and thread

"I think part of the beauty of our relationship with jewelry is that it can change and evolve as we do ourselves."

— Erika Christensen

1 Thread a needle on a comfortable length of thread. Leaving a 10-in. (25cm) tail, work in ladder stitch:
A. Pick up four 8º seed beads, and sew through the first two 8ºs again, so the beads form two columns. Reinforce the work by sewing through all the beads again.
B. Pick up two 8ºs, and sew through the previous pair of 8ºs. Sew through the new pair again.
C. Pick up two 11º seed beads, and sew through the previous pair of 8ºs. Finish by exiting the last two 11ºs you added.

2 A. Pick up an 11º and an 8º. Sew down through the adjacent column of 8ºs, and sew up though the following column.
B. Pick up two 8ºs, and sew down through the final column of 8ºs.
C. Sew through the previous two 8ºs (in the ladder you made in step 1) and continue diagonally through to exit the top end 8º.

3 A. Pick up two 8ºs. Sew down through the next 8º.
B. Pick up a 15º seed bead. Sew up through the next 8º.
C. Pick up an 8º and an 11º. Sew down through the existing 11º.

4 A. Pick up an 11º. Sew up through the 11º you added in step 3C.
B. Pick up an 11º and an 8º. Sew down through the next 8º.
C. Pick up a 15º. Sew up through the next 8º.
D. Pick up two 8ºs. Sew down through the next 8º.
E. Pick up an 11º and an 8º. Sew up through the last 8º you added in step 4D. Repeat steps 3–4 until you reach the desired length, ending and adding thread as needed.

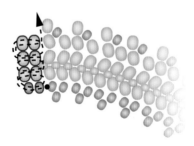

5 After you reach the desired length, stabilize the last two rows by sewing through them following a ladder stitch thread path. Do not add any beads at this point.

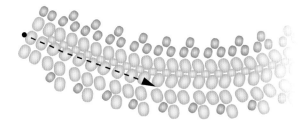

6 Attach a new thread about 60 in. (1.52m) long, and exit the tenth 8º as shown.

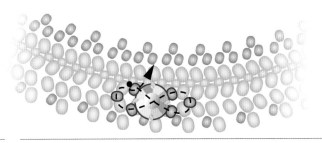

7 A. Pick up an 11º, rose montée, and 11º. Skip the next two 8ºs in the row, and sew through the following 8º in the row below.
B. Pick up an 11º. Sew back through the adjacent 8º, pointing back to the rose montée.
C. Pick up an 11º. Cross back through the rose montée, through the free holes.
D. Pick up an 11º. Sew through the bottom-row 8º that is adjacent to the one your thread exited at the start of this step.
E. Pick up an 11º. Sew through the 8º your thread exited at the start of this step, exiting to face the rose montée you added, and the first 11º you added in step 7A.

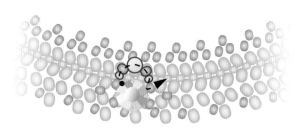

8 Pick up a 15º, 11º, 3mm pearl, 11º, and 15º. Sew through the next 11º.

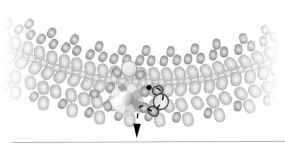

9 Pick up an 11º, 3mm pearl, and 11º. Sew through the lower 11º next to the rose montée.

Color Options

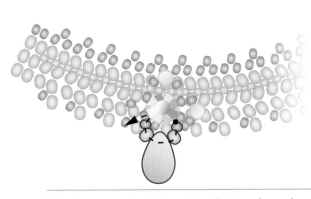

10 Pick up an 11º, 8º, drop, 8º, and 11º, and sew through the next 11º.

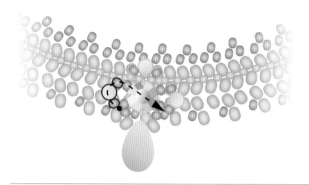

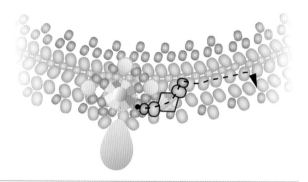

11 Pick up an 11º, 3mm pearl, and 11º. Sew through the above 11º, and continue into the rose montée and the following 11º.

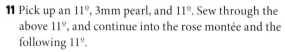

12 Pick up an 11º, 8º, 4mm bicone crystal, 8º, and 11º. Skip three 8ºs on the necklace, and sew through the next five 8ºs in the middle row. (If you want to adjust the spacing of the rose montée motifs, you can do it in this step.)

13 Repeat steps 7–12 to the end of the necklace. Once the last motif is placed, you can add as many rows as needed to even the edges. Then follow step 5 and finish the thread.

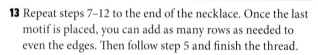

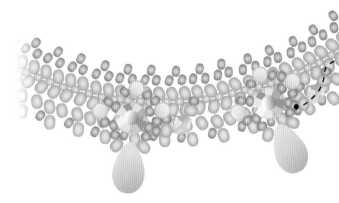

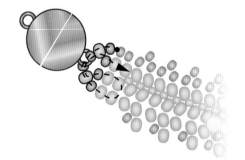

14 Attach a new thread about 10 in. (25cm) long. Exit an end 11º along the inside edge. Pick up an 11º, 8º, 11º, half of the clasp, 11º, 8º, and 11º. Sew through the last two 8ºs along the opposite edge and sew back through the next two 8ºs. Pick up an 11º, and sew through the 8º, 11º, clasp, 11º, and following 8º. Pick up an 11º, and sew through the next two 8ºs in the work. Reinforce by sewing through all the beads again. Finish the thread. Repeat on the other side to attach the second half of the clasp.

Aorra
Pendant

SUPPLIES

 .5g 15º seed beads

2g 11º seed beads

2g 8º seed beads

8 MiniDuo beads

9 4mm bicone crystals

 1 22x30mm oval fancy stone

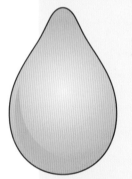 1 11x18mm drop bead, vertical hole

 2 O-Beads

 2 13x18mm pressed glass leaf beads, side-hole

Beading needle and thread

"Jewelry is the most transformative thing you can wear."

— Iris Apfel

1 Thread a needle on a comfortable length of thread, and pick up a MiniDuo bead, two 11º seed beads, an 8º seed bead, and two 11ºs, eight times. Sew through the beads again, and tie a surgeon's knot. Continue through the beads to exit the next 8º.

2 Pick up three 8ºs, sew through the 8º you just exited, and continue through the beads in the ring to the next 8º. Repeat around the ring. Finish by exiting the marked 8º.

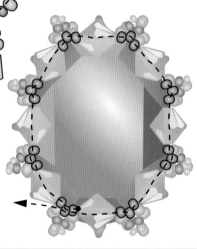

3 Insert the fancy oval stone face up. Pick up a 15º seed bead, 11º, 8º, 4mm bicone crystal, 8º, 11º, and 15º. Sew through the next 8º. Repeat around the ring. Finish by exiting the first 4mm bicone crystal you added.

4 Pick up three 11ºs. Sew through the next 4mm bicone crystal. Repeat around the ring. Finish by exiting the second 11º you added at the start of this step.

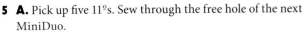

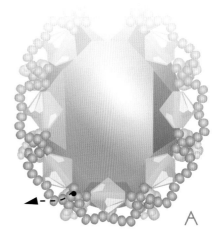

5 A. Pick up five 11ºs. Sew through the free hole of the next MiniDuo.
 B. Pick up five 11ºs. Sew through the next middle 11º in the set of 11ºs between the 4mm bicone crystals.
 C. Repeat steps 5A–B around the ring. Finish by exiting the 11º exited to begin this step.

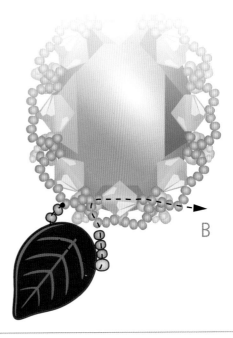

6 A. Continue through the next three 11ºs.
 B. Pick up two 11ºs, a leaf bead, 8º, and three 11ºs. Sew up through three 11ºs from the five added in step 5. Sew through the next 11º, 4mm bicone crystal, and 11º. Continue through the next four 11ºs, as shown.

7 Pick up two 11ºs, a leaf, 8º, and three 11ºs. Sew up through three 11ºs from the five you added in step 5. Sew through the next 11º, 4mm bicone crystal, and 11º. Continue down through six 11ºs and the following 8º.

8 A. Sew through the beads to the back side. Exit the marked 8º. Pick up nine 11ºs, and sew through the opposite 8º, two 11ºs, MiniDuo, two 11ºs, and the following 8º.

B. Pick up nine 11ºs. Sew through the opposite 8º, two 11ºs, MiniDuo, two 11ºs, and the following 8º. Sew through all the marked beads to reinforce the threads.

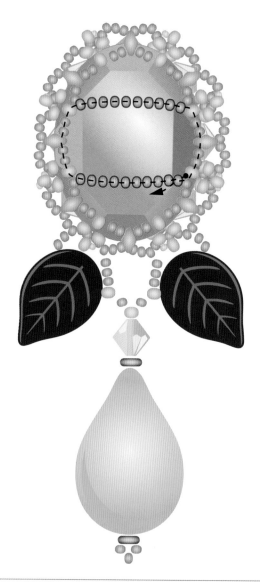

9 Sew up through the beads. Exit the upper MiniDuo. Pick up six 11ºs, and sew back through the MiniDuo. Sew through all the beads to reinforce. Finish the thread.

Color Option

Gallery

About the Author

Isabella Lam, who lives and works in Haifa, Israel, started as a beadwork designer and instruction writer. Beadwork became her profession over the years, and she enjoys exploring and creating new designs for beaded off-loom jewelry. Using new beads in unique combinations is always a wonderful challenge for her. She loves mixing tiny seed beads with spectacular sparkling Swarovski crystals for results that are fresh and unique. Isabella enjoys sharing her passion and love for beads, and she also inspires her students to share her love of jewelry making. She is known for her new thinking with endless possibilities.

Her designs have appeared in magazines, books, and shows. She has published many instructional articles in magazines and books over the years, including *Bead&Button* magazine, *Creative Beading* volumes, *Perlen Poesie* magazine, *Marcia DeCoster Presents*, and *To Catch a Crystal*. Her first book, *Beautiful Beadweaving: Simply Gorgeous Jewelry* was published by Kalmbach Books in 2017.

Because Isabella is a leading beadwork designer who has taught in the United States and Europe, fans all over the world have the opportunity to learn and create many of her off-loom projects.

If you are interested in giving beads a try, Isabella will help you create elegant and unique beadwork jewelry which will most certainly get you noticed. Her designs are wearable and give a great upgrade to every outfit for every occasion. Visit her web pages, www.isabellalam.com and www.etsy.com/shop/bead4me, or her Facebook pages, www.facebook.com/lamisabella and www.facebook.com/IsabellaLamdesigns/.

Thanks and Acknowledgments

Although I had plenty of encouragement over the years from family, students, friends, and beaders, I was only dreaming of ever writing a second book. All I needed was to believe in myself. As with my first book, I truly enjoyed the beading process and writing journey. My wonderful editors from Kalmbach Books made it come true for me once again.

I want to thank my amazing husband, Avi. He encouraged me to write another book of my newest designs. He cheers my spirit with endless patience, a lot of coffee, and great advice. He is a true believer.

I also want to thank my dearest friend, Hanni Hilf. She was always there with good advice and encouragement.

Experiments
with
SOUND

Isabel Thomas

raintree

Raintree is an imprint of Capstone Global Library Limited, a company incorporated in England and Wales having its registered office at 7 Pilgrim Street, London, EC4V 6LB – Registered company number: 6695582

www.raintree.co.uk
myorders@raintree.co.uk

Edited by Clare Lewis and Amanda Robbins
Designed by Steve Mead
Picture research by Eric Gohl
Production by Victoria Fitzgerald
Originated by Capstone Global Library Ltd
Printed and bound CTPS in China

ISBN 978 1 406 29030 1 (hardback)
18 17 16 15 14
10 9 8 7 6 5 4 3 2 1

ISBN 978 1 406 29042 4 (paperback)
19 18 17 16 15
10 9 8 7 6 5 4 3 2 1

British Library Cataloguing in Publication Data
A full catalogue record for this book is available from the British Library.

Acknowledgements
We would like to thank the following for permission to reproduce photographs: NASA: 16; Newscom: Minden Pictures/Pete Oxford, 15, Reuters/Stringer, 18; Shutterstock: Andrey_Popov, 10, Bryan Brazil, 22 (right), Monkey Business Images, 11 (bottom)

All other photographs were created at Capstone Studio by Karon Dubke.

We would like to thank Patrick O'Mahony for his invaluable help in the preparation of this book.

Every effort has been made to contact copyright holders of material reproduced in this book. Any omissions will be rectified in subsequent printings if notice is given to the publisher.

All the Internet addresses (URLs) given in this book were valid at the time of going to press. However, due to the dynamic nature of the Internet, some addresses may have changed, or sites may have changed or ceased to exist since publication. While the author and publisher regret any inconvenience this may cause readers, no responsibility for any such changes can be accepted by either the author or the publisher.

Safety instructions for adult helper
The experiments in this book should be planned and carried out with adult supervision. Certain steps should *only* be carried out by an adult – these are indicated in the text. Always follow the instructions carefully, and take extra care when using scissors (p12) and glass bottles (p24). Never poke fingers or any other object into your ears. Never make loud noises near your ears. The publisher and author disclaim, to the maximum extent possible, all liability for any accidents, injuries or losses that may occur as a result of the information or instructions in this book.

Contents

Some words are shown in bold, **like this**. You can find out what they mean by looking in the glossary.

Why experiment?

Why is space silent? How can blue whales hear each other hundreds of kilometres apart? Why do some animals have enormous ears? You can answer all these questions by investigating sound.

Scientists ask questions like these. They work out the answers with the help of **experiments**.

Get your ears, eyes and hands ready! You'll need to **observe** your experiments carefully and record what you hear, see or feel.

An experiment is a test that has been carefully planned to help answer a question.

The experiments in this book will help you to understand what sound is and how it behaves. You'll learn how to work like a scientist, and have lots of fun along the way!

IS IT A FAIR TEST?

Most experiments involve changing something to see what happens. Make sure you only change one thing, or **variable**, at a time. Then you will know that it was the variable you changed that made the difference. This is called a fair test.

WARNING! Ask an adult to help you plan and carry out each experiment. Follow the instructions carefully.
Look out for this sign.

ADULT
HELP

Follow these steps to work like a scientist.

Ask a question.

Come up with an idea to test.

Plan an experiment.

What will you change?
What will you keep the same?
What will you measure?

Make a **prediction**.

Observe carefully.

Work out what the results mean.

Answer the question!

What is sound?

Sounds are made when something **vibrates** (moves to and fro). The vibrations are passed through the air as **sound waves**. When the vibrations reach our ears, we hear them as sounds.

FEEL THE SCIENCE ⬇

Turn on a radio and hold a balloon near the speaker, without touching it. Can you feel vibrations?

The speaker vibrates backwards and forwards. As it moves, it pushes the air around it. This air is squashed out of the way, and pushes the air next to it. The vibrations are passed on from one part of the air to the next. When they reach the balloon, they make the balloon and the air inside vibrate, too.

Sound waves move through the air a bit like pressure from your hands moves through a slinky. Stretch a slinky out on a table, between your hands. Move one hand back and forth to squash the end of the slinky. The squashed area moves along the slinky as a wave, but each coil only moves back and forth in the same place.

You hear sounds when sound waves reach your ears. The vibrating air makes your **ear drums** vibrate. Your ear turns these vibrations into signals that are sent to your brain.

Rest your hand on your throat while you speak. Can you feel vibrations?

REAL WORLD SCIENCE

Musical instruments make air vibrate in different ways. This is why they sound so different. To make an instrument you need something that vibrates when you tap, pluck, blow or scrape it. The vibrations are passed on through the air to our ears.

Make a rice pop bop

Sounds are made when something **vibrates**. We can't always see the vibrations, for example when a mobile phone rings. Can you prove they are there?

EQUIPMENT

- A mobile phone
- Large glass jar
- Plastic wrap
- Rice pops

Method

1 Set the mobile phone to ring with a musical or ringing tone (make sure the "vibrate" mode is turned off). Put the phone inside an empty glass jar.

2 Stretch a piece of plastic wrap over the top of the jar, as tightly as possible. This is the dance floor for your rice pop bop.

Scatter a few rice pops on the plastic wrap.

Predict: What do you think will happen to the rice pops when the phone rings?

4 Call the mobile phone so that it starts ringing. What happens to the rice pops?

 Repeat the **experiment**, turning up the **volume** of the phone each time. Does it change the way the rice pops dance? What happens if you use different dancers, such as grains of salt?

IS IT A FAIR TEST?

To make it a fair test, you should only change one thing at a time. When you change the volume of the phone, is the plastic wrap stretched just as tightly each time? How could you improve your experiment?

Conclusion

When something makes a sound, part of it must be vibrating. Sometimes the vibrations are very small and hard to see. When the phone speaker vibrates, the air next to it vibrates too. The vibrations are passed through the air and the sides of the container to the plastic wrap. The dancing rice pops help you to see the vibrations.

What makes sounds loud or soft?

Sound is a form of **energy**. When a sound passes through the air, energy is being transfered from place to place.

REAL WORLD SCIENCE

Sound energy can be changed into other forms of energy – and back again. This is useful. A microphone changes sound energy into **electrical signals**. These can travel further than **sound waves** without fading. A loudspeaker changes electrical signals back into sound waves.

Volume and vibrations

The loudness or softness of a sound is called its **volume**. The volume of a sound wave tells us how much energy it has. A loud sound makes the air **vibrate** more, so more sound energy reaches our ears. Smaller vibrations mean that less sound energy reaches our ears, and the sound is quiet or soft.

When you pluck an elastic band, you transfer energy to it. The harder you pluck, the more energy you transfer and the bigger the vibrations. Bigger vibrations make louder sounds.

As sound waves travel, their energy fades and the sound becomes quieter. Because louder sounds have more energy to start with, they travel further.

Sound energy is measured in **decibels**. Our ears can be damaged by too much sound energy.

REAL WORLD SCIENCE

A stethoscope focuses sound energy and sends it all in one direction, along a narrow pathway. This makes it possible to hear very quiet sounds, such as a heartbeat.

Turn up the volume

How can you make a quiet sound louder, and easier to hear? You could stand closer to the source, so the **sound waves** have more **energy** when they reach your ears. Is there another way?

EQUIPMENT

- Something that makes a very quiet sound, e.g. a ticking clock
- Sheets of A5, A4 and A3 paper
- Large, quiet room
- Tape measure or metre rule
- Sticky tape
- Scissors

Method

1 Stand next to the clock. Can you hear it ticking? Try moving a metre away. Can you still hear it ticking? How far can you go before you stop hearing the clock?

2. Roll the smallest sheet of paper into a cone. Make the smallest opening about 3 centimetres (1 inch) across. Use sticky tape to hold the cone together.

Predict: If you listen to the clock through the cone, will it sound louder, softer or the same?

3. Hold the smallest opening of the cone to your ear and listen to the clock. What do you hear? Does it sound louder, softer or the same? Move your head so that the cone points in different directions. Does this change how the clock sounds?

Don't put the end of the cone in your ear. Rest it just next to your ear.

4. Move one metre away from the clock, and listen again. Record how far you can go before you stop hearing the clock through the cone.

5 Make a bigger cone, using a sheet of A4 paper. Hold it up to your ear and listen to the clock again. Does it sound louder or softer? Record how far you can go before you stop hearing the clock.

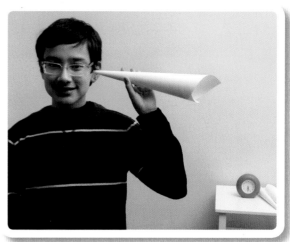

6 Make a cone using A3 paper. Use it to listen to the clock. Does it sound louder or softer? Record how far you can go before you stop hearing the clock through this cone.

7 Use a table like this to record your results. This will make it easier to compare them.

Hearing device	Distance when you stop hearing the clock (metres)
None	
Small cone	
Medium cone	
Large cone	

IS IT A FAIR TEST?

Remember to change only one thing at a time – the **variable** you are testing. Everything else should stay the same. Is the original sound always the same? Is each cone made from the same type of paper? Is the smallest opening always 3 centimetres across?

Conclusion

Sound **energy** from the ticking clock is passed through the air in all directions. Only a small amount of it reaches your ears. A cone-shaped "ear trumpet" gathers more **sound waves** than your ear can. As the sound waves travel down the cone towards your ear, their energy is combined. This **amplifies** the sound (makes it louder). Bigger cone ends gather more sound energy, so the sound is amplified more.

REAL WORLD SCIENCE

Hiding inside curled leaves helps these bats hear better. The leaves make a cone shape. Calls from other bats are amplified as they travel into the leaves. By the time they reach the bottom, sounds are up to 10 **decibels** louder!

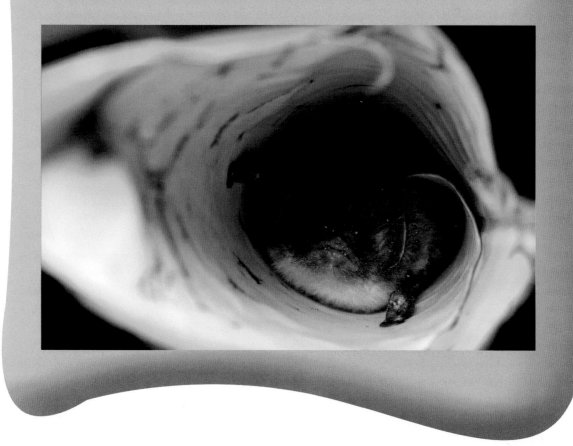

What can sound travel through?

Sound needs something to travel through. Most sound **vibrations** travel to our ears through air (a **gas**), but sound can travel through **solids** and **liquids**, too.

Sound can't travel in a **vacuum** such as space. There is no air to pass on the vibrations. If this spaceship exploded, the astronaut would hear almost nothing.

Hang a wire coat hanger on a long piece of string. Wrap the ends of the string around the first finger of each hand. Swing the hanger so that it taps a wall gently. What do you hear? Now hold the tips of your first fingers tightly against your ears. Swing the hanger so it taps the wall gently. What do you hear? Try this out with other objects.

When you tap the coat hanger, it vibrates and makes a sound. The way we hear the sound depends on which material the vibrations travel through to reach our ears.

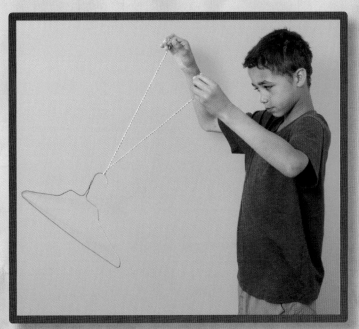

Sounds travel better through solids than gases. When the vibrations travel through air, not many of them reach our ears. The sound is quiet. When the vibrations travel through string, more of them reach your ears so the sound is much louder.

How fast does sound travel?

Sound travels at different speeds through different materials. It can travel much faster through **solids** and **liquids** than through air.

REAL WORLD SCIENCE

Sound travels faster in water than in air, so it can travel further before it fades. The loud sounds made by blue whales can be heard by other whales up to 1,600 kilometres (995 miles) away, which is like you standing in London and hearing someone speaking in Rome.

Make a telephone

Sound travels faster and further through **solids** than it does through **liquids** and **gases**. But do some solids transmit sound better than others? Find out by making a string telephone using different materials.

EQUIPMENT

- Two paper or plastic cups
- Two paper clips
- Different materials such as wool, string, thin metal wire, nylon fishing line, dental floss and cotton thread.

Method

1 Ask an adult to help you measure and cut a 10-metre length of wool. Ask an adult to make a small hole in the bottom of each cup. Push each end of the wool through a cup and tie it to a paperclip to hold it in place.

ADULT HELP

2 Have a friend hold one cup while you hold the other. Move apart until the wool is stretched tightly. Hold your cup to your ear while your friend speaks into the other cup. Can you hear them?

3 Ask your friend to choose ten words from a dictionary and speak them into their cup, in a quiet voice. Listen through your cup, and write down what you hear.

4 Repeat steps 1 and 3 using a different materials to join the cups.

Predict: Which material will be best at transmitting sound? Which will be worst?

Material	Predicted rank (1 = best at transmitting sound)	Number of words heard correctly	Actual rank
Air			
Wool			
Metal wire			

5 Use a table like the one at the bottom of page 20 to record your results. Analyse your results. Which material made the best telephone?

IS IT A FAIR TEST?

Make sure you only change the **variable** you are testing. This is the material used to join the cups. The length and tightness of each cord should be the same. Is it a fair test if each material is a different thickness? Is your friend speaking at the same **volume** each time? Is it a fair test if your friend says different words each time? How could you improve your **experiment**?

Conclusion

When you speak into your telephone, the **sound waves** travel from the first cup to the second cup through the cord. Sound travels better through cords made of **denser** materials such as metal wire. Softer materials, such as wool, **absorb** more sound than harder materials. The tightness of the cord also changes how well sound travels. Can you use this to explain your results?

What makes sounds high or low?

Two sounds can be the same **volume**, but sound very different. Sounds can be low like a lion roaring, or high like a monkey screaming.

The **pitch** of a sound describes how high or low the sound is. It is linked to the number of **vibrations** (or **sound waves**) that reach our ears every second.

High sounds have a high number of sound waves per second.

Low sounds have a low number of sound waves per second.

Anything that affects how quickly an object vibrates can affect the pitch of the sound it makes.

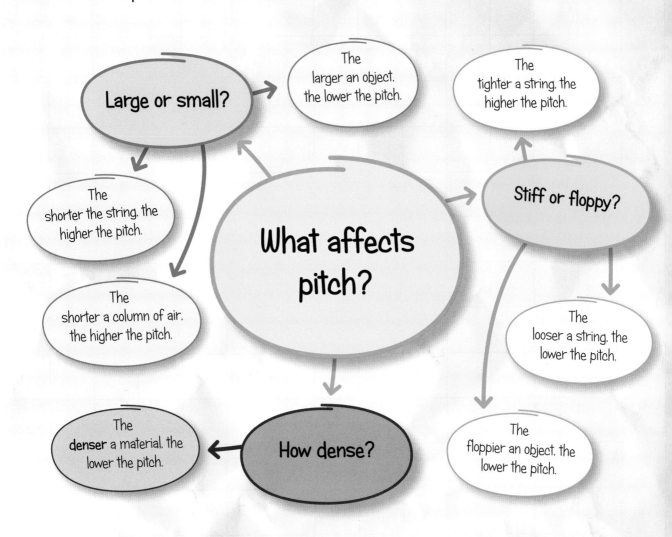

Large or small?

The larger an object, the lower the pitch.

The tighter a string, the higher the pitch.

The shorter the string, the higher the pitch.

What affects pitch?

Stiff or floppy?

The shorter a column of air, the higher the pitch.

The looser a string, the lower the pitch.

The denser a material, the lower the pitch.

How dense?

The floppier an object, the lower the pitch.

SEE THE SCIENCE ↓

Wrap two elastic bands around an empty box. Wrap one around the box twice so it is tighter. Pluck both bands. The tighter band wobbles more quickly. It makes a higher pitched sound.

Bottle band

Can you change the sound a bottle makes just by adding water? **Experiment** with changing **pitch** and make music.

EQUIPMENT

- Five empty glass bottles
- Measuring jug
- Water
- Wooden spoon
- Stickers numbered 1 to 5

Method

1 Fill one bottle with water and leave one empty. Pour a different amount of water into each of the others. This is your drum kit!

Predict: Which bottle will make the highest sound when you tap it, and which will make the lowest sound?

2 Put a sticker on each bottle to record your prediction – 1 for the bottle that you think will make the highest sound, and 5 for the lowest sound.

Glass can be dangerous if it breaks. Ask an adult to help you.

3 Tap the side of each bottle with a wooden spoon. What do you hear?

4 Line up the bottles in order of pitch. Was your prediction right? How can you make a note lower or higher?

IS IT A FAIR TEST?

The **variable** that you are changing is the amount of water in each bottle. Everything else should stay the same. Is it a **fair test** if the bottles are different shapes and sizes? Is it a fair test if they are standing on different surfaces? How can you improve your experiment?

5 Repeat the **experiment**, but this time blow across the top of each bottle instead of tapping it.

Predict: Which bottle will make the highest sound when you blow across it, and which will make the lowest sound?

6 Put a sticker on each bottle to record your prediction – 1 for the bottle that you think will make the highest sound, and 5 for the lowest sound.

7 Blow across the top of each bottle. What do you hear?

8 Line up the bottles in order of **pitch**. Was your prediction right? How can you make a note lower or higher?

Conclusion

When you tap the bottles with a wooden spoon, the glass and water **vibrate** together and make a sound. The fuller bottles have more **mass**, which wobbles more slowly. They produce lower sounds. The fullest bottle makes the lowest sound. The empty bottle makes the highest sound.

When you blow across the bottles, it is the air inside the bottles that vibrates to make the sound. A shorter column of air vibrates more quickly, so the bottles with most water make the highest sounds. The longer the column of air, the lower the **pitch**.

Plan your next experiment

Experiments have helped you discover some amazing things about sound. Just like you, scientists carry out experiments to answer questions and test ideas. Each experiment is planned carefully to make it a **fair test**.

YOU ASKED... ## YOU FOUND OUT THAT...

What causes sounds?

- Sounds are made when something **vibrates**. Sometimes the vibrations are too small to see.
- The vibrations make the air or material next to them vibrate too.
- The vibrations are passed through a material as **sound waves**.

What makes sounds louder and softer?

- Sound is a form of **energy**. The more energy a sound wave has, the louder the sound.
- The bigger the vibration, the louder the sound.
- A cone-shaped "ear trumpet" focuses sounds towards your ears, and **amplifies** them (makes them louder).

What can sound travel through?

- Sound can travel through different materials, including **solids**, **liquids** and **gases**.
- Sound travels through some materials better than others. This can be useful when you want to **muffle** a sound.

What makes sounds high or low?

- The **pitch** of a sound (how high or low it is) is related to the number of vibrations per second.
- Faster vibrations lead to higher pitch sounds.
- The tighter a vibrating string is, the higher the pitch of the sound.
- The larger a vibrating object is, the lower the pitch of the sound.

Experiments also lead to new questions! Did you think of more questions about sound? Can you plan new experiments to help answer them?

Being a scientist and carrying out experiments is exciting. What will you discover next?

Remember that loud sounds can damage your ears.

WHAT NEXT?

→ Do the vibrations change if you change the tightness of the plastic wrap. or the material of the container or dance floor? Plan an experiment to find out.

→ Does the material of the ear trumpet make a difference? Plan an experiment to find out.

→ How well do different materials **absorb** or reflect sound? Plan an experiment to find out. Hint: Try making headphones stuffed with different materials.

→ What happens when you change the length. thickness or material of a vibrating cord? Plan experiments to find out.

Glossary

absorb soak up

amplify make louder

analyse examine the results of an experiment carefully, in order to explain what happened

decibel unit used to measure the volume of a sound; can be written as dB

dense how tightly packed the matter that makes up a material is

ear drum part of the ear that vibrates when sound waves hit it

electrical signals small bursts of electricity used to send coded information

energy the power to make something happen

experiment procedure carried out to test an idea or answer a question

gas material that changes shape to fill its container, and can expand or be squashed so it takes up a different amount of space

liquid material that is runny and changes shape to fill the bottom of its container, but always takes up the same amount of space

mass the amount of matter making up an object or material

muffle stop sound travelling; make a sound quieter

observation noting or measuring what you see, hear, smell or feel

pitch how high or low a sound is

prediction best guess or estimate of what will happen, based on what you already know

solid material that is firm, does not change shape and always takes up the same amount of space

sound wave how sound travels through air

vacuum completely empty space

variable something that can be changed

vibrate move to and fro very quickly

volume how loud or soft a sound is

Find out more

Books

Bang! Sound and How We Hear Things, Peter Riley
  (Franklin Watts, 2012)

Earsplitters! The World's Loudest Noises, Steve Parker
  (A&C Black, 2009)

Making Noise! Making Sounds, Louise and Richard Spilsbury
  (Raintree, 2014)

Shhh! Listen! Hearing Sounds, Louise and Richard Spilsbury
  (Raintree, 2014)

Websites

www.bbc.co.uk/schools/scienceclips/ages/9_10/changing_sounds. shtml
Do online sound experiments – no equipment needed!

www.childrensuniversity.manchester.ac.uk/interactives/science/ brainandsenses/ear/
See inside your ears and find out how they hear sounds.

www.educationscotland.gov.uk/resources/s/sound/solid.
See how sound waves travel through a solid and a gas.

Index